HOW TO BREAK OUT
of an
ENGLISH RESIDENTIAL LEASE

5th Edition

Charles Boston

First Edition December 1993
Second Edition January 1995
Third Edition June 1997
Fourth Edition September 2003
Fifth Edition November 2020

Published by
Charles Boston
www.Boston Radford.com

How to Break Out of an English Residential Lease
5th Edition

ISBN 978-0-9530962-2-0

© Charles Boston

British Library Cataloguing-in-Publication Data
A CIP record of this title is available from the British Library.

Layout and typesetting in 10.5/14pt Times New Roman by Geoff Fisher
geoff.fisher@yahoo.co.uk

Foreword to the Fifth Edition

When the Labour government enacted the Leasehold Reform Act 1967, giving long leaseholders of houses (but not of flats) the right to acquire the freehold, little did the general public and the surveying and legal professions in particular realise what a complex area "Enfranchisement" would become.

Since this time these provisions have been extended, enhanced and, it could be argued, made more complex by the Landlord and Tenant Act 1987 and the collective enfranchisement provisions of the Leasehold Reform, Housing and Urban Development Act 1993 with the latter giving the right to collective enfranchisement and enhancing and extending individual rights. What makes this area both interesting and complex is the inter-relationship between the legal principles, the valuation principles and the ultimate "value" which can be achieved when an individual or collection of individuals pursue their enfranchisement claims.

In more recent times the sale by some housebuilders of only a long leasehold interest in the property to a purchaser has brought the whole area of long leasehold rights to the public's attention and highlighted the area as one for scrutiny. In the wider context, on 21 July 2020, the Law Commission published its long-awaited report on leasehold enfranchisement entitled "Leasehold home ownership: buying your freehold or extending your lease". Running to 841 pages, it contains detailed proposals but it remains to be seen whether they will reach the statute book.

Charles Boston is recognised as one of the leading valuation practitioners in the leasehold enfranchisement field. His experience and knowledge in the area is readily apparent and this fifth edition is to be welcomed.

Professor Del Williams BA, LLB, MCD, FRICS, MRTPI, MCIArb

September 2020

Introduction

The word "eccentric" is defined in the Oxford English Dictionary as "unconventional and slightly strange". This does rather sum up how the rest of world sees the United Kingdom. It must seem eccentric that we continue to give our citizens medals that refer to a long extinct "empire" and bestow upon others ancient titles that echo a time of heraldry. The way we embrace pageantry is also both splendid and extraordinarily eccentric.

Take our judiciary. Most countries require their judges to wear some degree of fancy dress, but no other country has their senior judges wearing a full-bottomed wig, together with a black silk damask gown, trained and heavily embellished with gold embroidery, over court coat, lace cuffs and jabot, black breeches, stockings and buckled shoes!

When it comes to real estate, or "property" as the English prefer to call it, our tendency to eccentricity does not desert us. Unlike every other developed country, where you either rent or own your property, we rejoice in the uniquely English system of leasehold tenure and it is, incidentally, an English system, not a British system.

In Scotland there is no such thing as leasehold. People either rent or they own and, if they own, they own the freehold. In Northern Ireland, whilst concepts of "Freehold Absolute" and "Good Leasehold" exist, they prefer a class of title called "Fee Farm Grant", which is essentially a hybrid between freehold and leasehold. Only in Wales do they share the English system of leasehold, but whilst much of the legislation is identical, there are nevertheless differences in the content and format requirements between England and Wales.

Many assume the leasehold system derives from the feudal system, which was introduced by William I, known, not inappropriately by the French, as "William the Bastard", following his victory at the Battle of Hastings in 1066. Actually the feudal system was abolished by the Tenures Abolition Act 1660, otherwise known as the Statute of Tenures, and it was many years later before the leasehold system, as we know it today, really began to take shape.

The Grosvenor family was amongst the first to develop it into a fine art. The head of the Grosvenor family is the Duke of Westminster, who owns the largest and most notable of the private landed estates in London. It is an interesting story how it came about. In 1667 Sir Thomas Grosvenor, who was a baronet, which is the first rung on the aristocracy ladder, married twelve year old Mary Davies. Nowadays that sort of thing would get you a rather lengthy prison sentence. In those days it was merely considered expedient, particularly as, in this case, Mary's family just happened to be significant land owners and the marriage resulted in Grosvenor receiving a dowry of around 500 acres of land. That land covered what is now known as Mayfair, Belgravia, Pimlico and part of Knightsbridge. It was not quite as good as it might sound, as the part now occupied by Belgravia and Pimlico was then mostly marshland and considered fairly useless, even for farming. Nevertheless, it was still quite a result.

The Grosvenor family prospered significantly as a consequence of this union with the Davies family and, over the next 150 years, the family title was progressively elevated. As a result, when a decision was made to develop this marshland in 1824, that decision was made by Richard Grosvenor, 2nd Marquess of Westminster. It brings to mind the exploits of Louis Mazzini in the wonderful 1949 film, Kind Hearts and Coronets, except that there is no suggestion that the Grosvenors had to murder their relations in order to work their way up the aristocratic ladder!

When it came to developing this land, Grosvenor commissioned the most celebrated builder of the time, Thomas Cubitt, on the basis that if anyone could make something out of this marshland, Cubitt could. So Cubitt took on this huge project and, over a period some thirty years, until his death in 1855, created some of the greatest and the most admired architecture in London. However, when it was all completed, rather than selling the buildings in the normal way, Grosvenor came up with the idea of selling long leases.

Many people today find it extraordinary that most of Central London is still owned by such people as The Duke of Westminster, Earl Cadogan, Viscount Portman, Baron Howard de Walden, The Duke of Bedford, The Earl of Ilchester and Baron Phillimore. Apart from these ancient titled families, other areas in Central London, such as Bayswater and Victoria, are owned by The Church Commissioners for England and of course the area around St James's and Regents Park is owned by the title that trumps them all, the Crown.

The rest of the world may marvel at what they see as eccentricity, but these landed estates have helped to create the greatest city in the world. The mechanism of a managed estate ensures that areas of the city are maintained at a consistently high level. The example of Pimlico is often cited. Pimlico was developed by Cubitt for the Grosvenor family at the same time as Belgravia, but the Grosvenor family sold Pimlico in 1953 to help pay for the old Duke's death duties. Since this time Belgravia has continued to be maintained to a high standard and Pimlico, by comparison, has deteriorated.

The Roman philosopher Lucretius once proclaimed *"Vitaque mancipio, nulli datur, omnibus usu"* (Life is given to none freehold, but it is leasehold for all). Given that none of us lasts forever, that is a depressingly valid observation, but when it comes to leasehold property, the good news is that expiration is by no means inevitable. There have been several Acts of Parliament designed to allow leaseholders to take action to prevent their investment deteriorating. Such laws allow owners of houses to buy their freehold and owners of flats to buy lease extensions or participate in buying the freehold of their building.

However, sorting out a system to give leaseholders these rights has proved to be fraught with complications. It has resulted in around twenty parliamentary revisions since the original Leasehold Reform Act 1967 and more than a thousand case precedents determined either by the valuation tribunals or the law courts. Most of these case precedents have provided clarification where it was needed and direction where the legislation has lacked both clarity and direction.

The Leasehold Reform Act 1967 was the first significant Act of Parliament allowing owners of long residential leases to buy their freehold. Unfortunately it only applied to houses and only small houses at that. It was heralded, according to the original green paper, as an Act intended to help, "the deserving poor". Actually its main purpose was to get Jim Callaghan re-elected into his South Wales constituency. It was at least successful in that respect, but it failed in just about every other respect.

In 1974 a Conservative Government decided to increase the scope of eligibility and allowed owners of more valuable houses to buy their freeholds. That still excluded owners of the most valuable houses and excluded everyone who owned a flat. It was not until 1993 that the Leasehold Reform, Housing and Urban Development Act removed value limits on houses and, for the first time, gave flat owners rights to extend their lease or to club together to buy the freehold of the block.

However, the 1993 Act had provisions that still excluded some properties on account of their ground rent. This was improved with a rather short sighted provision in the Housing Act 1996. It was not until a further amendment in the Commonhold and Leasehold Reform Act 2002 that qualification was finally made simple. In future, it said, any property would qualify providing only that it was held on a long lease, this being defined as a lease with an original term in excess of 21 years, and that the owner had owned it for two years.

In their enthusiasm to iron out the wrinkles, Parliament scrapped the single most valid justification for eligibility, which was that the property, whether it was a house or a flat, had previously to be the claimant's sole or principal residence.

This amendment immediately opened the flood gates to property companies and private investors, who could make multiple claims in a way that was entirely contrary to the justification or, as some might have seen it, the *casus belli,* of the original legislation.

This led to a new question that needed to be asked: what is a house? When a house needed to qualify as someone's home, the answer was self-evident. But when there was no need to show that it was a home, questions arose as to whether a Georgian terrace building obviously constructed as a house, but now used as an office, was a house for the purposes of this legislation. It seems clear that, in their rush to simply things, Parliament threw out the baby with the bath water. The wrinkles were ironed out, but it no longer made any sense.

But what about Commonhold you might ask? The answer is that, despite twelve years of preparation at the Lord Chancellor's office, it was received with about as much enthusiasm as Nigel Farage at the European Parliament. In 2019 the principal of Mortgages Policy at UK Finance stated that Commonhold was "fairly reasonable and functioning", which is an extraordinary statement. In the eighteen years since its enactment there have so far been no more than about twenty commonholds created. It may be a reasonable form of property tenure, but it certainly is not functioning!

Despite the largely unsatisfactory state of affairs, there has only been one Act of Parliament relating to leasehold enfranchisement that has entered the statute book since 2002; that is the Leasehold Reform (Amendment) Act 2014. One of the smallest Acts of Parliament ever written, it simply provided that in future it was not necessary for a claimant under the 1993 Act to sign the initial notice. Instead it could be signed by a solicitor or surveyor acting on behalf of the claimant. In other words 1993 Act claims could henceforth be treated in the same way that 1967 Act claims had always been treated.

Leasehold enfranchisement legislation has involved a series of really quite badly drafted and badly conceived statutes extending over a period of half a century. It is not surprising that there are disputes relating to the value of a property, but what is surprising is the number of disputes relating to the intention or interpretation of a statutory provision. In Sweet & Maxwell's Handbook of Residential Tenancies, for which I am the chief editor, there are more than a thousand cases that we have digested, mostly from the Upper Tribunal (Lands Chamber) and the Law Courts. Leasehold enfranchisement is a much larger subject than most people might reasonably imagine.

In 1993 I published the first version of this guide under the somewhat prosaic title "Understanding Leasehold Enfranchisement". In 1995, 1997 and 2003 I published new editions which followed various changes in the law as well as landmark decisions in the tribunals and law courts. Whereas this current guide is based on those previous editions, I have widened its scope considerably and, in view of these changes, although this is effectively a fifth edition, I have decided to change the title to "How to Break out of an English Residential Lease", which is really the point of it all.

But there are moves afoot to try once again to sort things out. On 21 July 2020, the Law Commission published their proposals for reform which may be summarised by their introductory statement: *"We are recommending the retention of the existing enfranchisement rights, but in an improved, streamlined form."* The published document is extremely wordy, encompassing no less than 841 pages. On 30 September 2020, Professor Nick Hopkins, Commissioner for Property, Family and Trust Law, broadcast the Blundell Lecture under the title *"Making our homes our own: The Law Commission's Reports on Residential Leasehold and Commonhold"*.

The general conclusion of the Law Commission is that leasehold, as a form of property tenure, does not work and "where freehold is possible, it is preferable to leasehold". Despite the abject failure of commonhold to be adopted since 2002, the Law Commission is keen to promote it. Commonhold, Professor Hopkins pointed out, has several advantages over leasehold. For a start it is not subject to the risk of forfeiture, making it a better form of collateral security. Furthermore, it does not involve the subservience of leasehold which, he said, had "never been designed to deliver ownership".

One further advantage of commonhold, he suggested, was that the commonhold association would own the common parts which would give them a valuable asset on which to raise finance for essential repairs. As a valuer, I cannot see how the common parts of any building could have any market value, but that is another matter.

The highlights of this report can be summarised in a little less than 841 pages as follows:

    a)   They recommend that the statutory lease extension, currently applying to owners of flats, should be extended to a new term of 990 years. They also suggest that those house owners, who currently have an option to claim a 50 year extension, could in future apply for a 990 year lease. With regard to flats, it is much more sensible for leaseholders to be able to acquire a virtual freehold lease, than merely a 90 year extension. But to extend this option to those with houses is really quite silly. First of all the existing 50 year extension is a right to remain at the house paying a "modern ground rent". It is not a lease extension in the normal sense of the term and there is no capital payment involved. See Chapter 4. But, apart from that, it is absurd to think that anyone who has the right to buy their freehold would choose instead to acquire a 990 year lease. There would be a negligible difference in the price and they would still not own their own home.

b) For owners of a "very long lease", they propose to allow leaseholders to buy out their ground without having to pay for an extension of their lease. Well that's fine, but if you have a "very long lease", although you may not feel the need to extend that term, the cost of doing so would be *de minimis* in any event, so this doesn't really offer any benefit.

c) With collective enfranchisement claims, they propose that the residential element should be reduced from 75% to 50%. The idea here is that flats above shops or offices would become eligible. But the problem here is that, in order to buy the freehold, the residential tenants would have to buy the commercial elements in the process and that would make it largely unviable, so I cannot see this being a practical benefit.

d) They also recommend abolishing the provision relaying to a resident landlord. At the moment with a building containing no more than four flats, one of which is occupied by the freeholder, providing that freeholder has lived in the building before it was converted into flats (a 2002 Act modification) that freeholder can resist a claim by the other tenants to acquire the freehold. It seems to me that, if you have a house which has been in the family for several generations and you need to down-size, converting the house into flats in order to be able to remain at the same address is a reasonable thing to want to do. Accordingly it seems fair to allow that freeholder to retain ownership of the house, but the Law Commission evidently didn't think so.

e) One proposal which seems quite sensible is to allow the parties in a dispute which is limited to valuation issues only, to refer the matter to a single member of the First Tier Tribunal, who will act as a sort of honest broker in determining the correct price. This would be given the trendy new name of a "Alternative Track" method.

f) They have been a bit radical when it comes to costs – these being the legal and valuation costs for which a landlord can seek reimbursement from their claimant. The Law Commission states that ***"If Government adopts a valuation methodology that seeks to reflect open market value for the property being acquired by a leaseholder"*** - and that,

I would have thought is a pretty big if – then the claimant should not be responsible for any "non-litigation" costs. It is obvious that, if the Government were to produce some sort of system which will make valuers redundant, then the landlord would not need to instruct a valuer to produce a valuation. Even so, they would still need to instruct a solicitor to deal with the notices. I cannot see any sensible way that the government could introduce a valuation methodology which would make sense and accordingly, this seems to be a fairly unlikely possibility.

g) They are proposing to abolish the two year ownership rule and also to abolish the one year rule applying to claims that are withdrawn. The former might be considered a good idea, but the latter is designed to prevent tenants from wasting landlord's time and, I would have thought, abolishing that is not such a good idea.

The main question which many leaseholders are asking is whether, if these proposals are enacted, it will be any cheaper and, if so, whether they should postpone making a claim until these proposals have become law. Well, the first thing to say is that there is no certainty that those proposals will become law. Equally there is no certainty that any legislation stemming from these proposals would make lease extensions or enfranchisement claims any cheaper.

One suggestion incorporated into these proposals is that the new legislation could set some sort of structure to determine capital values. Alternatively there could be limits on a claimant's liability to pay the landlord's legal and valuation costs. The former of these does seem extremely unlikely and I cannot see how it could really work in any sort of equitable way. The limit on landlord's costs is much more likely.

On the actual valuation side, the one area where it may become cheaper is in relation to the sort of leases which have sprung up in recent times. These are typically for a term of 125 or 150 years involving a ground rent which doubles every ten years or so of the term. Did you know that if you could fold a piece of paper 50 times the pile would reach the moon? You can't actually fold a piece of paper more than seven times, but this theoretical example just shows the effect of continued doubling. Similarly, if you take a flat worth £250,000 sold on a lease of 125 years, subject to a ground rent of £200 pa which doubles every ten years, the amount of that ground rent will exceed the value of the flat long before the lease has expired. Such ground rent provisions are clearly iniquitous and any landlords who have incorporated such provisions into their leases should not be surprised if their actions give rise to new legislation which prevents them from continuing to exploit their tenants in this way.

In considering whether any legislation that derives from these proposals is going to make things cheaper, it is worth appreciating that there were very few measures in the Leasehold Reform, Housing and Urban Development Act 1993 or the Leasehold and Commonhold Act 2002 that had any effect on the price. The 1993 Act was principally about giving flat owners rights they had never had before and the 2002 Act was an attempt to simplify things and establish some consistency. These Acts were therefore mostly about rights; they were not about valuation.

In 1992 I was on a Committee set up by the Council of Mortgage Lenders to advice the Government during the formation of the 1993 Act. I was invited by the CML to join a similar committee during the formation of the 2002 Act. On both occasions it was suggested that the new legislation might incorporate fixed leasehold to freehold relative values for different length leases. On both occasions I pointed out that, if you fixed relative values, you would also have to set out in the Act how those relative values would be affected by different ground rent obligations. You might also have to allow for the fact that a short lease in the centre of London might have a different relative value to freehold as compared to a short lease somewhere else. The committee acknowledged these points and concluded that it would be best to leave it to the valuers.

In conclusion, if these proposals are ever enacted, it seems unlikely that there will be any significant changes to the price that a claimant would need to pay, either to extend their lease, or to acquire their freehold. And, for the avoidance of doubt, even if commonhold does become more popular, no one is suggesting that tenants could become commonholders without first enfranchising. The only probable difference is that there may be a few more options to explore. As a result, rather than simplifying matters, it seems inevitable that there will be just as many opportunities, complications and difficulties.

I hope that this guide will provide a helping hand to all those who find themselves immersed in the eccentric English leasehold system.

Charles Boston FRICS

London, SW1

Contents

1   What is a Residential Lease?

The short answer is that it is a legal document that gives you the right to live in a residential property for a certain number of years. Indeed a lease is defined in law as "a term of years absolute". You might ask what the point is of buying a property where, after a certain number of years, you can be chucked out. The answer is that it depends largely on how long the term of the lease is, how much you are being asked to pay for it and what the rights and obligations of that lease might be.

1.1   **Types of leases** - Leases can come in all shapes and sizes. The term, or length, of a lease is perhaps the single most relevant aspect. The most common term for a lease is 99 years, which derives from an historic common law provision which ruled that 99 years was the longest term a lease could be. Today, although many leases are still granted for a term of 99 years, there is no statutory limitation and the more common terms of lease tend to be 125 or 150 years. There are also leases for 999 years, which are often referred to as "virtual freeholds".

It is only leases with an original term of more than twenty-one years that are eligible for protection under either the 1967 or 1993 Acts. This is what the law refers to as a "long lease". Leases for a shorter period are sometimes granted in circumstances where the landlord wishes to prevent their tenants from making a statutory claim against them. In some cases, such as in Eaton Square, Eaton Square Properties Ltd (a subsidiary of the Grosvenor Estate) grants leases of 20 years but also gives the tenants a right to restore their lease to its original term at any time.

Both "long leases" and these twenty year leases need to be distinguished from may be referred to as "rental leases". These are more correctly described as a "tenancy agreement" or "rental agreement" and usually subject to an Assured Shorthold Tenancy, commonly abbreviated to an "AST". These tenancy agreements are subject to the provisions of the Housing Act 1988, which allow a landlord to let their property for a term of between six months and two years without their tenant acquiring security of tenure. As this book is concerned with leasehold enfranchisement, I shall not delve further into rental agreements.

As leases are for a specific number of years, it follows that they begin to reduce in length from the moment they are granted. They can therefore have any number of years left when you come to buy them or, to be more accurate, when you take an assignment of them. The important thing, therefore, is to pay a price that reflects the value of what you are actually buying. It may seem that the leasehold system suits landlords more than tenants, but actually it provides a great deal of flexibility for those who buy them. In simple terms it allows you to buy a more valuable property than you might otherwise be able to afford, if initially you accept a shorter term of occupation.

A lease with around fifty years unexpired may, for example, be worth around three quarters of its equivalent freehold value. So if you come across your ideal house held on a lease with fifty years unexpired, you can probably buy it for twenty-five per cent less than you would have to pay if it were offered as a freehold.

Of course settling for a short lease term can be something of a Faustian solution, as you will then have a depreciating asset and, when it eventually reaches expiry, it will have no value. Worst of all, it may even have a negative value if, on expiry, the property is in any way dilapidated, as you may then have both to vacate the property and pay for its restoration.

That, at least, is how it would be if it were not for the fact that there are laws which enable you to extend your lease (in the case of a flat) or buy your freehold (in the case of a house). These laws allow you to transform a wasting asset into a brilliant investment, paid for in stages at a time to suit you. I will look at the opportunities to extend a lease or "enfranchise" it in later chapters, but first it is helpful to be aware of what rights and obligations are contained within a lease.

1.2   **Ground rents** - One thing which leases have to contain is a ground rent. In 1776 the Scottish economist, Adam Smith, wrote an essay entitled "An Inquiry into the Nature and Causes of the Wealth of Nations" in which he said *"The rent of a house may be distinguished into two parts, of which the one may very properly be called the Building-rent; the other is commonly called the Ground-rent."*

That may have been the case in 1776, but today ground rents have nothing to do with the rental value of the ground. In most cases they are simply an opportunity for a landlord to get something for nothing. The official reason why ground rents continue to exist is due to a requirement in English law that, for every contract, there must be "consideration". You might think that if one person gives another person a million pounds and the other person hands over the keys to their property that is "consideration" enough. But the thing about leases is that they involve an enduring obligation and accordingly the law considers that they require an enduring consideration. That, at least, is the rather tenuous explanation one is given.

Ground rents can vary enormously. On the one hand you get the quaintly innocuous ones which provide for a peppercorn, or a red rose on midsummer's day "if demanded". On the other hand, leases can be a few hundred pounds, doubling periodically throughout the term of the lease, or geared to a percentage of capital or rental value.

Most estate agents' property particulars either fail to mention the ground rent or simply mention the current ground rent. It is essential to establish, not just what the current ground is, but what provision there is to increase or review that rent during the currency of the lease, as these provisions can be extremely onerous. I was asked recently to provide expert evidence in a case of professional negligence where somebody had bought a flat for less than £200,000 but with a clause that provided for the ground rent to double every ten years of the term of 150 years. In the last ten years the ground rent was scheduled to have risen to nearly £3,000,000 pa.

The Government is currently considering new legislation which will make it illegal to incorporate any ground rent in a new lease. Due to the enduring contractual need to show "consideration", new leases may be subject to a peppercorn, but even that may be considered unnecessary in the future. Like most good intentions it is unlikely to happen that quickly and it is unlikely to affect existing leases.

1.3   **Covenants** - Apart from ground rents, leases contain a great many obligations, known as "covenants". The covenants which impose a duty on the landlord are very small in number and mostly implied. With a single house there really isn't anything a landlord is required to do other than to provide "quiet enjoyment" and not to "derogate from the grant". In the case of a block of flats, the landlord must also make sure it is managed and insured.

The tenant, on the other hand, has few rights and a great many obligations. Covenants fall into two categories: positive and restrictive. Positive covenants are those which require you to do something and restrictive covenants are those which prevent you from doing something. English law has long held that restrictive covenants can be enforceable on a freehold transfer, but positive covenants cannot. So, for example, if you have a large garden, you can sell half of it on a freehold basis subject to a restrictive covenant preventing the new owner from building on it. What you cannot do is require the owner to mow the lawn once a fortnight. You could if you sold them a lease, but not if you sold them the freehold.

The position was clarified in 1848 by a landmark case called *Tulk v Moxhay*. It concerned the sale of Leicester Square, which was sold with a covenant requiring it to be kept as an open space. The developers who bought it thought they were being rather clever arguing that to "keep something as an open space" was a positive covenant and, as such, was unenforceable. The court ruled that it is the effect of a covenant that counts, not the way it is worded and the effect of this covenant was quite clearly intended to restrict any development on the site. Accordingly it was held to be an enforceable covenant, which is why today Leicester Square is still a square and not some horrible Victorian development.

Freehold covenants, like freehold itself, are not time limited and sometimes one comes across covenants created a long time ago and the rationale for their existence may no longer be justified. Those adversely affected by such a covenant may apply to have that covenant lifted or modified under section 84 of the Law of Property Act 1925. It is a fairly arduous process which involves making an application to the Upper Tribunal (Lands Chamber) and then waiting the best part of a year before they will consider the matter. In most cases, it is best to enter into a dialogue with whoever now has the benefit of the covenant, if indeed there is any benefit. It may mean having to pay some modest amount to have the covenant extinguished, but it will still probably be cheaper and quicker than referring the matter to the Upper Tribunal.

Since the nineteenth century leases have increased enormously in length and complexity in order to incorporate an ever increasing number of covenants which lawyers have thought up over the years. Initially leases, or "indentures", as many types of legal documents were known, were often limited to one or two pages, such brevity being encouraged by the fact that they had to be hand written. A modern residential lease by comparison will typically contain more than forty pages covering complicated ground rent provisions, extensive repairing obligations, limitations on how you can use the property and limitations on your ability to assign or sub-let the property. Some covenants appear vaguely far-fetched, prohibiting the use of a property as an auction or a brothel. Some covenants are actually quite helpful, such as "mutual enforceability", which allows the tenant to sue the landlord for failing to enforce a covenant against a neighbour in the same building.

Then there are covenants which can represent something of an ambush. These might include a covenant which would provide that, if the tenant should become bankrupt, the landlord can "forfeit" the lease, which means that they can revoke the lease and take back the property. This sort of covenant is often hidden away at the back of a lease, beyond where most people are inclined to read. However, this is just one example of the need to scrutinise a lease thoroughly as a "bankruptcy clause", as this is known, can have a substantial effect on the value of that lease, rendering it largely unmortgageable.

It is quite common to hear reference to a standard fully repairing and insuring lease. There is no such thing. Different landlords may, at different times, have their own standard form of lease, but leases vary enormously and can be more or less restrictive, more or less onerous and more or less practical. As a result, it really is necessary to read beyond the first few pages.

1.4   **Reasons to enfranchise or extend the lease** – The term "enfranchise" refers to that process of unshackling yourself from the restrictions and obligations of a lease. It is often used to refer to the process of acquiring a lease extension, but that is not technically enfranchisement. The new lease, although ninety years longer and with no ground rent, will still contain the same restrictions and obligations as the old lease. Enfranchisement is when you acquire the freehold and that right is limited to houses or entire blocks of flats.

Although there are many advantages in owning your own freehold, acquiring a lease extension in the case of a flat is still a very sensible way to protect the investment and, should it apply, to eradicate an onerous ground rent provision. Moreover, it is worth remembering that you can apply for a second ninety year extension as soon as you have completed the first.

The fact is leases are a wasting asset and they reduce in value exponentially as they approach expiry. Take a lease with an unexpired term of 45 years. That is probably an unmortgageable lease and it will be losing value exponentially every year. On the other hand, if it is extended by the statutory term of 90 years, it will become a lease of 135 years and that is unlikely to see any depreciation for at least forty years.

However, you might wonder why it is that Parliament did not give owners of flats the right to acquire virtual freehold leases of 999 years. I made precisely this point when I was advising the Council of Mortgage Lenders in 1992. The Green Paper we were asked to comment on provided for an extension of 80 years. I suggested that this was far too short given that the aim was surely to put flat owners in an equivalent position to house owners. My objection was relayed to the Government, who responded a week later saying that they would be prepared to increase the term to 90 years. They felt that 90 years was really quite long enough. It appears that the penny has finally dropped with the Law Commission who have at last proposed virtual freehold leases as an option. It remains speculation as to whether this will ever be law.

In the case of an actual enfranchisement it is a matter of upgrading from leasehold to freehold. Freehold is clearly a superior form of ownership, indeed the highest form of ownership one can have in England. Whereas a lease is defined as "A Term of Years Absolute", freehold is defined by as "Tenure in Fee Simple Absolute in Possession". The word "fee" in this context is derived from fief, meaning a feudal landholding. Feudal land tenures existed in several varieties, most of which involved the tenant having to supply some service to his overlord, usually in the form of soldiers. When feudal land tenure was abolished all fiefs became "simple", without conditions attached to the tenancy. In other words they were no longer a tenancy.

Neither of those legal definitions is really very helpful. The real difference comes down to fundamental ownership. If you have a lease, even one that is for a term of 999 years, your ownership is limited to the envelope, or "demise", of that lease. So if you should want to enlarge the property in any way you will need to agree this with the freeholder, who will be the owner of the airspace and the subsoil. Furthermore, if you should want to make any substantial alterations within the demise, it is usually necessary to obtain the landlord's consent and, depending on the terms of the lease, the landlord may have an absolute right to oppose the plan or to charge a fee for consenting to the plan and that charge may be entirely at their discretion.

Those who own their freehold only have to obtain consent from the local Town Planning Authority or possibly English Heritage if their property is listed. Moreover, the General Development Order gives you a free range to carry out a fair amount of development without even consulting the planners.

Many purchasers are distrustful of the leasehold system and will only buy freehold. Even the words "landlord" and "tenant" are something of a deterrent to many purchasers, who may feel it is ignominious to pay £1,000,000 for a property and then be referred to as a "tenant". There is an understandable reluctance to accept that one is beholden to some faceless *soi-disant* "lord of the land". Furthermore, leases are not "sold" by the landlord, they are "granted". It is as though someone buying a leasehold property should be expected at all times to doff their cap and show due deference to their freehold lord and master.

In summary there are many reasons to enfranchise. Leases are both restrictive and authoritarian, they are a diminishing asset and, compared to freehold, they are like travelling Economy Class. That doesn't mean they are a bad thing to buy; it just means that you need to view them as the first stage in a process. The next chapters will explain how you take it to the next stage.

2 Qualification and procedures for enfranchisement of houses

The 1967 Act was the first major piece of legislation to give leaseholders the right to enfranchise. The Act described itself as *"an Act to enable tenants of houses held on long leases at low rents to acquire the freehold or an extended lease"*. It was therefore restricted purely to houses and provided no rights to owners of flats, maisonettes or any kind of commercial property. Moreover, as the stated intention of the Act was to help *"the deserving poor"*, it excluded all houses above a certain value.

Since 1967, the law has been changed by over a dozen Acts of Parliament and various Statutory Instruments and Regulations and as the rules on qualification and valuation are so complex, I have given each its own chapter. This chapter will look at the rules on qualification and the following chapter will deal with the valuation issues.

2.1 **The property must be a house** - This is defined in Section 2 of the Leasehold Reform 1967 Act and has been revised in more than half a dozen cases referred to the courts, many of which have ended up at the House of Lords, now known as the Supreme Court.

 2.1.1 **The statutory definition:**

> ***Section 2(1)*** – *"For purposes of this Part of the Act, 'house' includes any building designed or adapted for living in and reasonably so called, notwithstanding that the building is not structurally detached, or was or is not solely designed or adapted for living in, or is divided horizontally into flats or maisonettes: and -*
>
> *a) where a building is divided horizontally, the flats or other units into which it is so divided are not separate 'houses', though the building as a whole may be, and*
>
> *b) where a building is divided vertically the building as a whole is not a house though any of the units into which it is divided may be."*
>
> ***Section 2(2)*** – *"References to this Part of this Act do not apply to a house which is not structurally detached and of which a material part lies above or below part of the structure not comprised in this house."*

2.1.2 **Houses with a non-residential element** - Early cases such as *Lake v Benett QB 1970* focused on such issues as to whether a building was a house for the purposes of the Act if it comprised a corner shop with an upper part where the leaseholder lived. The court found that such a building should be accepted as a house, notwithstanding its commercial element.

This decision was developed in 1982 when the House of Lords heard an appeal, *Tandon v Trustees of Spurgeons Home,* where it was ruled that, for a mixed use building to be a house, at least 25% of the building had to be used for residential purposes.

However, when the Commonhold and Leasehold Reform Act 2002 abolished the need for the house to be the claimant's sole or principal residence, it became more difficult. When, previously, a house had to be the claimant's sole or principal residence, the test was relatively simple. The tenant either lived there or he didn't, but when that test no longer applied, it was a matter of going back to examine the underlying intention of section 2.

In 2008 the Court of Appeal looked at the eligibility of a virtually derelict terrace building in Mayfair. The case was *Boss Holdings Limited v Grosvenor West End Properties Limited* and the property was a mid-eighteenth century terrace building in Mayfair It had obviously been constructed as a residential property, but this was arguably an anachronistic use, as all the surrounding buildings were now used as offices. If it had been used for residential purposes at the date of claim, the case would never have gone to court. On the other hand, if it had been used for office purposes, given the dilemma that was created by abolishing the residency test and the wording of section 2, it might still have gone to court with a fair chance of succeeding. As it was, although the building was now better suited for office purposes, it was not actually being used for anything. As a result, the Court of Appeal accepted the claim.

A year later another 1967 Act claim was made on a similar Georgian terrace property. The case was *Prospect Estates Limited v Grosvenor Estates (Belgravia) Limited* which related to a building occupied for both office and residential purposes. On appeal the claim was rejected on the basis that the predominant use was commercial and not residential. This was somewhat creative given that section 2 makes no reference to the user at the time of the claim.

This left a lot of people extremely confused as to what now constituted a house for the purposes of this legislation. The dilemma was addressed in 2012 by a Supreme Court appeal relating to two claims: *Day v Hosebay Ltd* and *Howard de Walden Estates Ltd v Lexgorge Ltd*. The claimants argued that if a building was originally built as a house, and this was not in question, then it satisfied Section 2(1) and, as there was no question of failing to satisfy Section 2(2) – the need to be vertically divisible - it must qualify. The landlord argued that there were two aspects to Section 2(1), the more important being whether the property was a house *"reasonably so-called"*. The Supreme Court found in favour of the landlords. These appeals were intended to clarify once and for all what criteria needed to be satisfied. Unfortunately, it was a somewhat sloppy decision and it did not provide anything like the sort of clarity that is required.

2.1.3   **Vertical division** - Subsequent cases looked at the provision in Section 2(2) where a qualifying property was required not to have a *"material part"* that *"lies above or below part of the structure not comprised in this house"*. The big question was what exactly constituted a "material part". Perhaps inevitably different courts reached different judgments. The current authority on this issue is a House of Lords case heard in 2002: *Malekshad v Howard de Walden Limited* which, overturning a previous Grosvenor case, ruled that a material part must actually be quite significant. This issue was looked at in another appeal on the Howard de Walden Estate only a year later. In *Collins v Howard de Walden Estates* a claim was made for two mews houses involving a fair amount of overlapping and the Court of Appeal again found in favour of the claimants, but again there is no categorical decision that can be relied upon in this respect.

2.2   **If it is not a house then it must be a flat** - In some instances a property may be considered a house by any normal person, but because a sufficiently significant part of the building runs under the next building or overhangs the property next door, it may fail the requirement to be vertically divisible as defined in Section 2(2). Some degree of overlapping is not necessarily a problem as has been stated in 2.13 above, but where the overhang is considered sufficient to render the property ineligible for a claim under the 1967 Act, the question then arises that, if it is not meet the legal requirement to be a house, does that make it a flat? For some time following the enactment of the 1993 Act, it was generally agreed that a property which failed to comply with section 2 of the 1967 Act must, by default, be flat. This position was finally confirmed in the 2002 Act.

2.3   **Rateable value limits** – The 1967 Act refers to rateable values which were abolished for residential property in March 1990. However, it is still necessary to have regard to these historic rateable values for the purposes of qualification, which will be discussed in more detail below.

2.4   **Minimum term of lease** – The lease must be for a fixed term which exceeds 21 years, even if determinable earlier. Section 64 of the 1993 Act amended the rules in respect of leases that could be determined by some unknown future event, such as the death or marriage of someone. Such leases are now treated as having long terms for the purpose of the Act.

2.5   **Linking leases** – For leases having a term not exceeding 21 years, it is important to be aware of the provisions of Section 3(3). These provide that, where a lease is granted out of the surrender of a previous lease, so that there is direct link between landlord and tenant, the commencement of the term will be the commencement of the earlier lease. Moreover, providing the link is intact, there could be a chain extending to any number of leases.

In order to qualify under the 1967 Act, the original lease must still have had a term in excess of 21 years. Accordingly, this provision does not mean that a lease of 20 years granted out of the surrender of an earlier lease of 20 years will be treated as a long lease. This provision is therefore only helpful in two circumstances:

First of all, if the current lease was granted for a term of less than 21 years, but was granted out of the surrender of a previous lease which <u>did</u> have a term in excess of 21 years, then establishing a link would enable a claim to succeed. Secondly, by establishing a link with a previous lease, you can consider any improvements carried out during the currency of the combined term. This may therefore allow the marginal value of an improvement carried out in the earlier lease to be disregarded.

It should be noted that this only applies to houses under the 1967 Act and there is no equivalent provision in the 1993 Act applying to flats and blocks of flats.

2.6   **Low rent -** Under Section 141 of the 2002 Act, it is no longer necessary to consider the amount of the ground rent. This must not, however, be confused with the need to check the ground rent as part of the investigation to determine which valuation basis applies (see below).

2.7   **Sole or principal residence -** The 2002 Act repealed the need for the house to be the claimant's sole or principal residence. Under Section 138 of the 2002 Act, it is merely required that the claimant, whether an individual or a company, has owned the house for 2 years.

2.8   **Shared ownership -** Generally, where there is shared ownership, none of the joint tenants is entitled to serve a valid leaseholder's notice of claim on their own. An exception to this is in the case of husband and wife. Where a property is owned jointly by a husband and wife and one dies, that remaining spouse may base a claim on the date of acquisition by the couple. However, where a house has previously been held in the name of, say, the husband and it is later assigned to the wife's name following a divorce, the wife would have to wait until she had owned the house for the statutory two year period before she could enforce a claim.

2.9   **Rights of trustees -** Section 6 of the 1967 Act provides that where a tenant occupies his house by virtue of a trust of which he is the sole beneficiary, in most instances he will be treated as occupying the house in right of the tenancy. The same provision is presumed to apply to ownership, now that Section 138 of the 2002 Act has changed the criteria in this respect.

2.10   **Successors in title -** Section 7 of the 1967 Act provides that where a tenant has died, having occupied the house as his main residence up to his death, any member of his immediate family who becomes a tenant of the house under the same lease will deem to benefit from the deceased's residency. Consequently if the deceased had lived in the house for, say, 6 months, the new tenant need only own the house for 18 months before being entitled to serve a notice.

2.11   **Assignment from a company to an individual -** There used to be considerable debate as to whether a landlord who opposed an assignment from a company to an individual was acting in contravention of Section

19(1) of the Landlord and Tenant Act 1927, which provides that an assignment cannot be unreasonably withheld. With the abolition of a residency test in Section 138 of the 2002 Act, such arguments have become largely, if not wholly, redundant.

2.12 **Grounds for a landlord to oppose a claim** – Certain landlords are exempt including: The National Trust (although the tenant may still apply for the 50 year extension providing the basis of valuation is Section 9(1) or Section 9(1A) – see below); the Crown (although they have agreed to act by analogy with the Act in most instances); registered housing associations and prescribed public authorities where the tenant is given the right to buy the freehold at a reasonable price.

2.13 **Grounds for opposing a notice** – apart from an assertion that the house does not satisfy the provisions of Section 2 (ie it is not a house), there are several grounds a landlord can cite in order to oppose a claim:

2.13.1 – **Family requirement** - A landlord can oppose a notice to enfranchise or to claim an extended lease if he can show that the house will be required for occupation by him or an adult member of his family as a sole or principal residence. The landlord's interest in the house must, however, have existed prior to 1 February 1966.

2.13.2 - **Development by landlord** – A landlord can resist a claim for an extended lease if he can demonstrate an intention to carry out a major development or redevelopment of the property that would require vacant possession. These grounds for opposition do not, however, extend to a claim for leasehold enfranchisement. Accordingly, if a tenant's claim for a 50 year extension is defeated in this way, he can counter-attack by serving a notice to buy the freehold after all.

2.13.3 **Development by public bodies** – Where the landlord is a public body that has already obtained consent to carry out a development within the next 10 years, the tenant will neither have the option to extend the lease nor to enfranchise.

2.13.4 **Compulsory purchase orders** – The house will be excluded if a notice for compulsory purchase has already been served by a qualifying local authority.

2.13.5   **Business tenancy** – A landlord can oppose a claim if the tenancy is a business tenancy subject to the provisions of Part II of the Landlord and Tenant Act 1954.

2.13.6   **Previous abortive claim** – If a tenant makes a claim and subsequently withdraws that claim the landlord is not obliged to admit any subsequent claim for at least one year. The change from two years to one year was introduced in the 2002 Act.

2.14   **Procedure to make a claim** - Unlike claims made under the 1993 Act, the claim notice is not referable to a specific section number but is referred to simply as a "Leaseholder's Notice of Claim". The notice may be signed by the claimant or by any duly authorised agent, typically a solicitor. These notices are fairly confusing and it is common for mistakes to be made. It is therefore best to use a solicitor who is familiar with the territory. However, if minor inaccuracies or omissions are made they will not usually invalidate a notice. There are two leading Court of Appeal authorities on this subject: *Speedwell Estates Lt v Dalziel* in 2001 and *Earl Cadogan v Strauss* in 2004 which sought to make clear the extent to which an inaccurate notice can still be valid.

2.14.1   **Clarification of intent** - The claim must first of all state whether it is a claim to acquire the freehold or to claim a fifty year extension.

2.14.2   **Proposal** - If the claim is to acquire the freehold, the claimant must specify the valuation basis which will apply under Section 9 (described in Chapter 3 of this guide). There is no requirement to propose a price, as there is with claims made under the 1993 Act.

2.14.3   **Statutory deposit** – The statutory deposit is equivalent to three times the ground rent, but there is no need to produce this until demanded by the landlord, when it may be required within 14 days.

2.14.4   **Deducing title** – With property that is registered, which is most property, this is a simple matter of producing a current Land Registry office copy of title. If a property is not registered, it is a matter of producing the deeds. Again there is no need to produce anything until so demanded by the landlord and the Act, which was passed at a time when many properties were not registered, allows for a period of 21 days.

2.15   **Completion** - The rules are contained in the Leasehold Reform (Enfranchisement and Extension) Regulations 1967. Under Section 6 of the Regulations, if completion has not taken place within one month from the date of agreement, the landlord may serve a completion notice requiring completion to take place on the first working day after the expiration of 4 weeks from the date of the completion notice.

If completion has not taken place within the period specified in the completion notice, the landlord may serve a further notice under section 10 requiring completion to be effected no later than two months from the date of this second notice. Also, under section 8, the landlord will be entitled to claim interest to be paid in lieu of ground rent on the agreed price at the rate of 2% above the Bank of England Base Rate.

If completion has not taken place within the expiry of the two months specified in the section 10 notice, the claim is deemed to be withdrawn. The landlord will then be entitled to keep the statutory deposit and claim all expenses under Section 9(4) of the 1967 Act.

3 Valuation bases for enfranchisement of houses

The original version of the Leasehold Reform Act 1967 specified rules for qualification and the valuation principles that would apply. The previous chapter addressed the question of whether or not a property may qualify for enfranchisement under the 1967 Act. This chapter will address the question of which valuation basis will apply if they do and I shall begin by clarifying the original basis, which still applies if a property meets the necessary criteria.

3.1   **The original 1967 Act basis** - The valuation basis prescribed in the original 1967 Act followed on from the original Green Paper, which stated that, whereas it was recognised that the land belonged to the landlord, the house itself should be regarded as belonging "in equity" to the tenant. The corollary to this was that the tenant should only be required to pay a price in respect of the land, excluding any value attributable to the house standing on that land.

This was clearly very tenant friendly and reflected the extreme socialist government of that time, a time when "unearned income" was taxed at 98%. But it became even more tenant friendly with an amendment contained in Section 82 of the Law of Property Act 1969. This provided that the tenant should not be treated as a "special purchaser" and there was therefore no need for the tenant to pay any additional amount in respect of marriage value.

The original value basis is contained Section 9(1) with that proviso contained in section 82 of the 1969 Act taken into account. In keeping with the underlying philosophy, the enfranchisement price is based on three things:

3.1.1   The capitalised value of the ground rent

3.1.2   The value on reversion of a "modern ground rent" for a term of fifty years, and

3.1.3.   The market value of the reversion thereafter.

3.2   **Determining the modern ground rent** – The modern ground rent is defined in Section 15 and is subject to a term of 50 years with just one review after 25 years. It is typically derived by first establishing the "entirety value" of the house (see below) and then applying a percentage of that entirety value to reflect the value of the site. Once the site value is established it is then a matter of applying an appropriate yield for a term of fifty years subject to one rent review after twenty-five years.

3.3   **Entirety value** – The idea of an entirety value is intended to be the most valuable property that could stand on the existing site. For example, in *Cadogan Estates Limited v Hows and Hock* (1988) the Lands Tribunal overturned the previous decision of the Leasehold Valuation Tribunal by ruling that the entirety value of a mews house in Belgravia was to be valued as a three storey house, although the actual house was two stories. The basis for this ruling was that other neighbouring houses had added another floor and it was felt that this further development was feasible both from an economic and a town planning viewpoint.

3.4   **Site value** - There are 3 established ways of arriving at the value of the site:

    3.4.1   The "cleared site" approach – This is usually applied where the house is nearing the end of its economic life and is therefore ripe for demolition. The approach is to look at the site for development purposes, having regard to local planning regulations and policies, and to value it on a comparative basis with similar sites sold for development in the vicinity;

    3.4.2   The "new for old" approach – This involves carrying out a residual valuation to show what it would cost to construct a new building in place of the existing, allowing for the normal costs of development, including a developer's profit. This is hardly ever employed as it is generally recognised that such valuations incorporate so many variable aspects that it is possible for 2 valuers to arrive at widely different conclusions;

    3.4.3   The "standing house" approach – This is by far the most common method for two reasons. First, there is often no helpful evidence of similar size sites being sold on the open market. Secondly, the existing building will already represent something close to a full development of the site. The aim then is to arrive at the value of the site by reference to the most valuable conversion, enlargement or refurbishment that would be allowed within the constraints of the user covenant and local planning regulations.

3.5   **Criteria for satisfying Section 9(1)** – In order to claim the benefit of Section 9(1), two criteria have to be satisfied:

3.5.1   The house if it is in London must have a Rateable Value as 31 March 1990 not exceeding £1,000 (£500 elsewhere), 31 March 1990 being the last day residential property was included in a Valuation List. The authority for this date is Statutory Instrument No. 434 which was issued in 1990 and Schedule 15 to the Leasehold Reform, Housing and Urban Development Act 1993. If the house did not have a rateable value as at 31 March 1990, the criterion is to have an equivalent rental value not exceeding £25,000 per annum (£16,233 elsewhere).

3.5.2   The ground rent at the date of claim must not exceed two thirds of the Rateable Value of the house on the "appropriate day", which is 23 March 1965 or the first day thereafter when the house appears on the Valuation List or, if the house did not appear on any Valuation List, then the equivalent letting value. This criterion is subject to a proviso whereby, if the lease was granted between 31 August 1939 and 1 April 1963, the ground rent must be no more than two thirds of the letting value at the commencement of the lease.

3.6   **The 1974 Act basis** - This category was introduced by Section 118 of the Housing Act 1974 and initially referred to houses whose rateable value exceeded £1,000 in Central London (£500 elsewhere), but did not exceed £1,500 and £750 respectively as at 1 April 1973. It was called Section 9(1A).

As with Section 9(1) valuations, the applicable date for considering the rateable value has been changed by Schedule 15 to the 1993 Act to the 31 March 1990. For houses that did not appear in the Valuation List at this time, the test is to have a rental value not exceeding £25,000 per annum. There are two inconsistencies in Section 9(1A):

3.6.1   Parliament evidently considered a letting value of £25,000 per annum equivalent to a rateable value in the 1973 Valuation List of £1,500. However, there is an inconsistency in relation to the lower bracket. With the rateable values it is taken at two thirds, so that instead of £1,500 it is £1,000. However, where the letting value applies, it is not two thirds of £25,000, which would be £16,666, but it is £16,233. This can only logically have been a mistake in the drafting, but it is law until the Secretary of State amends it, which seems unlikely.

3.6.2   As will be shown below, the valuation basis for Section 9(1) is based on an entirely contrived socialist principle. On the other hand, the valuation basis for Section 9(1A) is based on market principles. Despite this, if a house qualifies for a Section 9(1A) valuation, it can, as an alternative, claim a fifty year extension where the principles of Section 9(1) apply. This option does not apply to houses subject to Section 9(1C).

3.7   **Enfranchisement price under section 9(1A)** - Unlike Section 9(1), where the valuation only looks at the land value, with Section 9(1A) valuations, the tenant is required to pay a price for the entire building based on open market valuation principles. There is no assumption to value the property as though it had been developed to its maximum advantage, nor even to value it as though all the repairing covenants in the lease had been observed. If the property is dilapidated, then that is how it is to be valued. When one of the criteria for qualification was that the claimant had to be in residence at the time of the claim, it could be assumed that the building was at least in a habitable state. Since that requirement was abolished by Section138 of the Commonhold and Leasehold Reform Act 2002 a property in any condition may qualify.

Where a house is dilapidated, valuing it in its current state will of course result in a lower enfranchisement price than would be the case if the house were not dilapidated. The corollary to this is that a landlord might be able to support an action for damages on the basis that the tenant's failure to comply with the repairing covenants has resulted in the landlord losing money. In practice this is generally accepted as an unnecessary legal action and the usual solution accepted by tenants' valuers is to value the house in a "tenantable" condition, which is a provision specifically incorporated into Schedule 13 to the Leasehold Reform, Housing and Urban Development Act 1993, this being the valuation basis for the lease extension of flats.

3.8   **Improvements** – If the property has been improved by the tenant or any of his predecessors in title since the commencement of the term, the marginal value attributable to those improvements is to be disregarded from the valuation. This provision is often misunderstood by tenants.

It is quite common for a purchaser to carry out a complete modernisation of a house, including re-wiring, re-plumbing and sorting out any ingress of damp. Most of such works are likely to fall into the category of what has been termed "periodic maintenance", being works required under the repairing obligations contained in the lease. If a house requires a substantial amount spending on it, it may be presumed that the purchaser would have paid a price that fairly reflected this.

Most works which may be considered improvements may, under the terms of the lease, have required a licence. The tenant may therefore be required to produce that licence to counter any suggestion that they are in breach. There are perhaps three types of improvement:

3.8.1   Works to enlarge the property – these may include adding a rear conservatory or building an additional floor;

3.8.2   Changing the nature of space – for example converting a wet coal cellar into a dry utility room;

3.8.3   Carrying out an interior finish which is above and beyon the obligations of the lease and which has enhanced the market value of the property.

3.9   **Section 9(1B)** – Section 9(1B) allows a tenant to make an application to the Inland Revenue under Schedule 8 to the Housing Act 1974 for a certificate indicating what the Rateable Value given in the Valuation List would have been if improvements carried out by the tenant, or their predecessor, which have been taken into account in arriving at that Rateable value, were to be disregarded. In this way it may be possible to achieve the much more favourable Section 9(1) valuation basis. Very few practitioners today are familiar with this process, although it is still perfectly valid.

3.10   **Section 9(1C)** - Introduced by Section 66 of the 1993 Act, this relates to houses whose Rateable Value or equivalent rental value exceed the limits for Section 9(1A). The specific directions are contained in Schedule 15 to the 1993 Act and is essentially the same as Section 9(1A), but whereas tenants with houses that fall into Section 9(1A) may have security of tenure on the expiry of their lease, those with houses that fall into Section 9(1C) will have no such protection and this may therefore impact on the value of the reversion.

3.11   **Treatment of rent reviews** – Many leases contain rent reviews allowing the ground rent to be revised to a figure based on the open market capital or rental value of the property. Such clauses may allow the landlord to value the property with the benefit of tenants' improvements. However, in *Cadogan Estates v Sharp* (1998) the Lands Tribunal determined that for the purposes of the statutory valuation, all rent reviews should be assumed to relate to the property in an unimproved condition equivalent therefore to the vacant freehold value applied to the reversion.

3.12   **Marriage value** – Section 82 of the Law of Property Act 1969 established that no marriage value was payable for valuations under section 9(1). Otherwise for leases with less than 80 years unexpired, marriage value it is payable and under section 145 of the 2002 Act, it is to be shared equally between landlord and tenant.

3.13   **Leases with more than 80 years unexpired** – Section 146 of the 2002 Act provides that there shall be no marriage value payable in respect of leases having an unexpired term at the date of valuation exceeding 80 years.

3.14   **The effect of statutory protection** – Initially these claims were determined by valuing the landlord's reversion as the right to receive a "Fair Rent" as provided for under the Rent Act 1977. This approach was later changed following a Lands Tribunal decision in *Lloyd-Jones v The Church Commissioners for England* (1982) in which it was decided that this approach was inappropriate. That was because evidence showed that most tenants did not in fact hold over but were prepared to negotiate for a surrender and renewal of their lease before its expiry.

3.15   **The Lloyd-Jones methodology** – As a result of the above, it was decided that the better approach was to look at the vacant possession value of the house, rather than the potential income stream, but to discount that vacant possession value to reflect the risk, or likelihood, of the tenant holding over. In *Lloyd-Jones* the discount awarded was 10%. However, that discount must be understood to have reflected both the circumstances of the case and the evidence presented to the tribunal. The circumstances in *Lloyd-Jones* were a house in Maida Vale with an unexpired term of some 12 years where the contingent statutory protection would have been the Landlord and Tenant Act 1954, Part I. That in turn provided that a lessee would be entitled to a tenancy under the Rent Act 1977. Subsequently discounts as high as 25% have been agreed or determined by the tribunals in circumstances where the contingent protection was referable to the 1954 Act and the unexpired term was less than 1 year.

3.16 **The appropriate percentage today** – Section 186 and Schedule 10 of the Local Government and Housing Act 1989 have changed the position by providing that with any lease expiring after 15 January 1989, the tenant will no longer be protected by the 1954 Act. Instead they will be eligible for an Assured Periodic Tenancy (APT), as provided for in the Housing Act 1988, which basically provides that the tenant should pay the full market rental value of their property. In reality, while an APT rent is higher than a Fair Rent, it is still lower than a full market rent, if only due to the exclusion of any value attributable to tenants' improvements in the annual rent.

As an example of how such risk is currently valued, I have agreed discounts of 10% in Hans Place, Knightsbridge, where the unexpired term was approximately 12 months. Had these leases been subject to the protection of the Rent Act 1977, 1 would have expected to achieve discounts of 20% or more, but the reduced detriment to the landlord's reversion (due to a potential APT) coupled with the very short unexpired term resulted, somewhat by coincidence, in being consistent with the percentage adopted in *Lloyd-Jones*.

In an Upper Tribunal decision, *Clarise Properties Ltd's Appeal* (2012) the question arose as to what discount should be applied to the freehold reversion in circumstances where the valuation basis was Section 9(1). The statutory valuation provided for a fifty years extension and, with a current term of 28.5 years, that meant a final reversion in 78.5 years when it was assumed the tenant would be entitled to protection as an Assured Tenant. Despite the remoteness of this the Upper Tribunal determined that the reversion should be discounted by 20%, this then being known as the "Clarisse deduction".

3.17 **Procedure to make a claim**

3.17.1 Notice of leaseholder's claim – The tenant must serve a leaseholder's notice of claim on his landlord and all other persons having a legal interest in the property. This must be done using the appropriate form. Unlike the 1993 Act, the claim is not served under a particular section but is referred to simply as a "leaseholder's notice of claim".

3.17.2 Requirements pursuant to the notice – In reply the landlord may require:

> a) A statutory deposit – this is £25 or 3 times the current ground rent, whichever is the greater;

b) Evidence of title – with land registered at the Land Registry this is easily proven by deduction of the current office copy. Around 85% of all land in England is now registered. Of that 15% that remains unregistered, very little of it is leasehold, but for unregistered leasehold land it is a matter of referring to the deeds.

c) **A** statutory declaration - **it used to be necessary to provide a** statutory declaration in support of the claim that the property was the claimant's sole or principal residence. Since that requirement was abolished in the 2002 Act, this is no longer necessary.

3.17.3   **Landlord's reply** – The landlord has 2 months in which to oppose or admit the claim. In the event of the landlord being a head lessee the time limit can be extended to 4 months, but this is not commonly known and seldom applied.

3.17.4   **Landlord's failure to reply** – If the landlord should fail to respond in time, there are no real sanctions, but the tenant may then apply to the County Court to have the claim declared valid.

3.18   **Valuation examples -** At the beginning of this chapter, reference was made to the 3 bases of valuation. I shall now demonstrate the effect of each in turn:

In order to do this I have treated the house in each valuation example as having the same open market value of £800,000. It is held on a lease with 24 years unexpired subject to a current ground rent of £200 pa and there is provision for an increase to the current rent to an amount equivalent to 0.5% of the freehold value in 4 years. However, it is not quite so straightforward for 2 reasons:

3.18.1   **Development potential** – The property has scope for enlargement and if it were fully developed, it would have an open market value of £950,000.

3.18.2   **Tenant's improvements** – The current open market value of £800,000 takes into account some tenant's improvements which, if disregarded, would make the open market value £750,000.

There are therefore 3 open market values to consider:

i)   The open market value of the property as it now is, being £800,000;

ii)   The open market value of the property fully enlarged and developed, being £950,000;

iii)   The open market value disregarding tenant's improvements, being £750,000. We shall see how these factors are treated in each valuation example as follows:

3.19   **Valuation under Section 9(1)** - With Section 9(1) valuations it is necessary to arrive at the site value and we shall assume that the Standing House approach (see above) is to be applied. This requires the estimation of the "Entirety Value" and the matter of tenant's improvements does not have any bearing on the valuation.

Term for the next 4 years

Ground rent reserved	£200 pa		
YP for 4 years @ 6%	3.3651		
		£673	

Term until expiry

Estimated revised ground rent	£446 pa		
YP for 20 years @ 6%	11.4699		
Deferred 4 years @ 6%	0.7921		
		£4,052	
			£4,725

Reversion to Section 15 rent

"Entirety" value	£950,000		
Percentage attributable to site, say	40%		
Site value therefore	£380,000		
Yield on letting, say	4.75%		
Section 15 rent therefore		£18,050	
YP for 50 years @ 4.75%		18.9844	
Deferred 24 years @ 4.75%		0.3283	
			£112,498

<u>Reversion to perpetuity</u>

Current market value	£800,000
Deferred 74 years at 4.75%	<u>0.03226</u>
	<u>£25,808</u>
	£143,031

3.19.1 **Open market value** – It will be seen that the open market value of the house in the final tranche of the valuation is based on the present condition of the house. It is not appropriate to adopt the entirety value at this stage, which is only relevant in determining the Section 15 rent.

3.19.2 **Revised rent** – the revised rent is based on the unimproved freehold value, not the current market value, following the Lands Tribunal decision in *Cadogan v Sharp*.

3.19.3 **Adverse differential** – The investment yields employed to capitalise the income, to discount the future capital receipts and to determine the yield on the hypothetical letting of the site have all been taken at the same yield of 4.75%. Based on a ruling by Lord Denning MR, the decapitalisation and recapitalisation rates need to be the same to avoid what was described as an "adverse differential".

3.19.4 **Selection of yields** – The capitalisation rate of 6.0% selected here is intended to reflect the nature of this ground rent income, where it is fixed for fairly long periods and then subject to pre-determined increases. The deferment rate on the other hand derives from a case heard in 2007 called *Cadogan v Sportelli* where the Upper Tribunal prescribed a generic deferment rate for houses of 4.75%. This generic deferment rate has been the subject of many tribunal references where parties have argued that it should be different in different locations, with different length leases and with properties of a varying state of repair. In most cases the Upper Tribunal has taken the view that this rate should be the default position unless there are very compelling reasons. The sort of compelling reasons which have impressed tribunals are referred to 9.3 infra.

3.20 **Valuation under Section 9(1A)** - Where Section 9(1A) applies there are two principal differences. First, the reversion is based on the actual building, as opposed to the site. Also, providing the unexpired term is less than 80 years, the claimant will be required to pay marriage value.

Applying the same ground rent and values as in the previous example, this is how the valuation would look if Section 9(1A) applied:

<u>Term for the next 4 years</u>

Ground rent reserved	£200 pa		
YP for 4 years @ 6%	<u>3.3651</u>		
		£673	

<u>Term until expiry</u>

Estimated revised ground rent	£446 pa		
YP for 20 years @ 6%	11.4699		
Deferred 4 years @ 6%	<u>0.7921</u>		
		<u>£4,052</u>	
			£4,725

<u>Reversion to vacant freehold value</u>

Freehold value estimated at	£800,000		
Less value of improvements	<u>£50,000</u>		
Unimproved freehold value		£750,000	
Less 5% for risk of lessee holding over		<u>(£37,500)</u>	
		£712,500	
Deferred 24 years @ 4.75%		<u>0.3283</u>	
			<u>£233,914</u>
			£238,639

<u>Marriage value</u>

Unimproved freehold value (as above)		£750,000	
Less			
Value of lessor's interest	£250,950		
Value of lessee's interest at, say 51%	<u>£382,500</u>		
		<u>£633,450</u>	
		£116,550	
Amount due to the lessor		<u>50%</u>	
			<u>£58,275</u>
			£296,914

<u>**Say, £297,000**</u>

>   **3.20.1**   **Reflecting the right to hold over** – A 5% discount has been allowed to reflect the right to hold over in these circumstances. As stated above, this discount would vary according to the unexpired term of the lease and the evidence taken into consideration.

>   **3.20.2**   **Marriage value apportionment** – The marriage value has been split equally in accordance with Section 145 of the 2002 Act.

3.21   **Effect of Section 9(1) compared to Section 9(1A)** – Assuming the same house with the same ground rent obligations and the same market value, it can be seen that where the basis of valuation is Section 9(1) it would cost £143,000 but if that same house fell to be valued under Section 9(1A) the enfranchisement price would be more than twice this price at £297,000.

3.22   **Effect of Section 9(1C)** – Section 9(1C) is the basis of valuation introduced by Part I, Chapter III of the Leasehold Reform, Housing and Urban Development Act 1993. The valuation basis is intended to follow that contained in the Housing Act 1974, which introduced Section 9(1A). The one difference is that houses falling into the category of Section 9(1C) are also likely to fall outside the protection of Schedule 10 to the Local Government and Housing Act 1989, in which case there can be no valid argument for a discount to reflect the risk to the lessor of the lessee holding over on the expiry of the lease. Accordingly, in the above example, the enfranchisement price would be, not £297,000, but £304,500.

4   Criteria applying to lease extensions of houses

The provisions for a lease extensions applying to houses are significantly different to those applying to flats under the 1993 Act. The main difference is that the lease extension for houses is not a matter of acquiring a lease extension in the normal sense of the term. It is about acquiring the right to remain in possession for a further fifty years paying annually an amount which is intended to represent the rental value of the site on which the house stands. Furthermore, the "modern ground rent", as it is known, is subject to just one rent review after twenty-five years.

If that sounds completely alien to anything that happens in the real world, it is. Nobody ever rents a piece of land for building development for a period of fifty years and, if they did, they certainly would not agree to having just one rent review in the middle of that term. However, it was made part of the 1967 Act at a time when the aim was to protect the "deserving poor" by allowing them to hang on to their homes in some form when their leases ran out.

4.1   **Qualifying houses -** Any house that falls into the valuation bases Section 9(1) or Section 9(1A) can elect, as an alternative to enfranchisement, to have a 50 year extension. This right does not extend to houses falling into valuation bases Section 9(1B) or 9(1C). For houses in these valuation categories introduced in the 1993 Act, the only option is to buy the freehold.

4.2   **Terms of the new lease** – the first thing to appreciate is that the tenant does pay anything to acquire the fifty year extension. The payment comes in terms of an obligation to pay the modern ground rent which is determined and which kicks in when the old lease expires.

        4.2.1   **Duration of lease** – The new lease is for a term of 50 years from the expiry date of the original lease and it is effectively a reversionary lease. The process is quite different to the process involving a lease extension under Chapter II of the 1993 Act. With a 1993 Act extension, the old lease is revoked and replaced with a new lease which has no ground rent and endures for 90 years after the expiry date of the old lease. With a 1967 Act lease extension, the old lease is unaffected and the ground rent continues to be payable as before, but when that lease expires, there is then a rent review to determine the "modern ground rent" calculated in accordance with section 15(3).

4.2.2   **Rent** – The "Modern Ground Rent" is defined in Section 15(3) of the Act and is intended to represent the rental value of the site for a term of 50 years, subject to one rent review only after 25 years.

4.2.3   **No price payable** – There is no premium payable either at the time of the claim or when the Section 15 rent is determined, although the claimant is liable for the landlord's legal and valuation costs as provided for in section 9(4) .

4.2.4   **General terms of the statutory lease extension** – These follow the old lease with some specific modifications.

4.3   **Characteristics of the lease extension** – These lease extensions are not to be confused with those provided under the Leasehold Reform, Housing and Urban Development Act 1993 which apply to flats. Although it is a legal interest in property, it does not affect the enfranchisement price should the tenant subsequently wish to apply for the freehold (see 4.4 below). In some respects it is something of a Faustian solution where the tenant may feel that he has sorted out the erosion of the lease, but instead has been lulled into a sense of false security.

4.4   **Rights to enfranchise before the fifty year extension has started** – Any tenant who has elected to take a 50 year extension may subsequently elect to enfranchise. Before the 2002 Act, Section 16 of the 1967 Act provided that any subsequent enfranchisement claim had to be served before the old lease had expired. That was changed by Section 143 of the 2002 Act which allows tenants to enfranchise once the fifty year extension has commenced.

4.5   **Effect on subsequent enfranchisement price** - It might reasonably be thought that, once you have acquire a fifty year extension, that would make the house more valuable and it would make enfranchising less expensive. That was what various leaseholders on the Phillimore Estate thought in the early eighties. The houses all fell into section 9(1A) and they came up with this wheeze of applying for fifty year extensions and, before the ink had dried on their lease extensions, they applied to buy the freehold. The case, known as *Mosley v Hickman*, was heard by the Court of Appeal in 1986 who was bound to acknowledge that this was perfectly legal. However, the idea that you could get something for nothing in this way set off alarm bells. As a result, a few months later an amendment was rushed through Parliament in Section 23 of the Housing and Planning Act 1986. This provides that the enfranchisement valuation does not recognise any value to the fifty year extension.

5   Qualification and procedure for collective enfranchisement

Collective enfranchisement refers to the idea of a group of flat owners clubbing together to buy the freehold of their building. It was introduced for the first time in the Leasehold Reform, Housing and Urban Development Act 1993 and is the result of a lengthy series of amendments carried out between the first reading in Parliament in the autumn of 1992 and the Royal Assent some 10 months later. It became operative on 1 November 1993 and provides for the following:

5.1   **Qualifying buildings** – Section 3(2) of the 1993 Act provides that the building must be self-contained and, if not structurally detached, it must be capable of being *"redeveloped independently of the remaining of the building"*. It must also have its own services or be capable of having its own services without a substantial disruption to the building with which it is currently sharing them.

5.2   **Minimum number of flats** – Section 3(1) of the 1993 Act provides that at least two thirds of the flats in a building must have eligible leases (as defined below). Accordingly, where there are only two flats in a building, they must both have eligible leases.

5.3   **Non-residential element** – Section 4 deals with buildings in mixed use. Originally it provided that buildings would not qualify if their non-residential use, based on floor area, exceeded 10% of the total gross internal floor area. Section 115 of the 2002 Act increased this to 25%.

5.4   **Resident landlord** – Section 10 of the 1993 Act provided that a resident landlord may oppose a claim providing the building in question contains no more than 4 flats, including the resident landlord's flat. This provision is amended by Section 118 of the 2002 Act. In order to oppose a claim in these circumstances, a landlord must now show that he owned the building before it was converted into flats, and that he, or an adult member of his family, was in residence at that time.

5.5   **Exempted landlords** – A few landlords are exempted from the Act, such as charitable housing trusts and the Crown Estate. Despite this, the Crown, mindful of what happened to Charles I when he tried to be above the law, will usually admit claims by analogy to the Act.

5.6	**Qualifying leases** - The rules for determining a qualifying lease in Section 7 and Section 8 of the 1993 Act have been greatly simplified by the 2002 Act. It is no longer necessary to have any regard to the ground rent and the different rules for leases exceeding 21 years, but not exceeding 35 years, introduced in the Housing Act 1996, have all been scrapped. Since Section 117 of the 2002 Act, all you need to show is that the original lease term was in excess of 21 years.

5.7	**Quorum and residency requirement** - Again the rules were greatly simplified by the 2002 Act. The previous arrangement, set out in Section 13(2) of the 1993 Act, provided that two thirds of the leases had to be qualifying leases and, out of those, two thirds had to participate in the claim. In addition, 50% of those participating had to have resided in their flat for the previous 12 months. Section 119 of the 2002 Act abolished the provision in Section 13(2) whereby the initial notice had to be given by at least two thirds of qualifying tenants of flats contained in the premises.

Section 120 of the 2002 Act then abolished the further provision in Section 13(2) that "not less than one half of the qualifying tenants by whom the notice is given must satisfy the residency test" (being a matter of having resided at their flat for the previous 12 months). Accordingly, all that is left of Section 13(2) is a requirement that the number of lessees participating is at least 50% of the total.

5.8	**Procedure** – The procedure relating to a collective enfranchisement claim is fairly complex, requiring first of all the appointment of both a solicitor and a valuer who +will act for those lessees who have chosen to participate. Achieving a consensus on the appointment of those two professional advisers can be a problem in itself. It is then necessary to obtain a minimum of 50% participation and an agreement on how the non-participants will be funded. Once these objectives have been met the solicitor can incorporate a "Right to Enfranchise Company" and begin the process.

5.9	**Concept of "RTE" company** – It was felt that there needed to be a consistent form of company to act as the nominee purchaser for collective enfranchisement claims. The 2002 Act therefore introduced the concept of an "RTE" (Right to Enfranchise) company. This is defined as a private company limited by guarantee, whose purpose is to exercise the right to collective enfranchisement under the Act.

5.10	**Notice of invitation to participate** – Section 123 of the 2002 Act introduced a new Section 12A notifying all the qualifying lessees and inviting them to participate in the collective action through the mechanism of an RTE company. However, it should be appreciated that the Act does not require that every qualifying lessee is invited to participate and once the 50% quorum is met, those who have elected to participate can proceed without any reference to the others in the building. This strikes me as yet another flaw in the 1993 Act.

5.11   **Participation agreement** – section 14 of the Act sets out the requirement to detail who the participating lessees are and these are usually formalised in a participation agreement prior to the service of a claim notice.

5.12   **Claim notice** – The S.13 claim notice is to be served by the RTE company, as the nominee purchaser, according to regulations set out in the original Section 13 of the 1993 Act, as amended by Section 123 of the 2002 Act.

5.13   **Deposit** – Unlike the arrangement with individual lease extensions, there is no provision to pay a deposit with collective enfranchisement claims.

6   The valuation principles for collective enfranchisement

The valuation basis is defined in Schedule 6 to the 1993 Act and covers twelve and a half pages of small print. It is not appropriate in this guide to deal with every aspect of this, but the main elements may be summarised as follows:

6.1   **Valuation date** – Section 126 of the 2002 Act has amended the provisions contained in Schedule 6 to the 1993 Act and the valuation date is now the date of claim by the RTE company, as it has always been with Leasehold Reform Act claims.

6.2   **Open market value of freehold reversion** – The directions are contained in Section 3 of Schedule 6 and refer to various aspects that may need to be considered. These include the following:

    6.2.1   Full account is taken of all leasehold interests to which the freehold interest is subject.

    6.2.2   The landlord's interest is to be valued excluding any marginal value attributable to the Act. This is not to exclude the possibility of marriage value, where this applies, nor "hope value" where that applies (see below).

    6.2.3   Any incremental value attributable to improvements carried out by the current tenant and all predecessors in title is disregarded.

    6.2.4   All rights and burdens to which the freehold interest is subject are taken into account.

    6.2.5   Should there be any other factor, not specifically described in the previous sub-sections that may have an effect on the open market value of the freehold interest, which should also be taken into account. This will not apply in the event of any transaction which may have created a negative value.

    6.2.6   Any defects in the freehold title are to be taken into account in reducing the value of the freehold interest.

6.2.7   Apart from any voluntary leasebacks, there is the possibility of mandatory leasebacks as provided for in Section 36. Where this applies, it will be reflected in the valuation.

6.2.8   Any transaction carried out by the freeholder on or after 20 July 1993 (the date when the Act was passed), which may have the effect of increasing the open market value of the freehold interest, will be disregarded from the valuation.

6.3   **Landlord's share of marriage value** – Section 127 of the 2002 Act changed Section 4 of Schedule 6 to the 1993 Act by providing that marriage value should be shared equally in all circumstances where marriage value is an appropriate head of claim (i.e. for leases having unexpired lease terms at the date of valuation not exceeding 80 years – see below).

6.4   **Marriage value with very long leases** – Section 128 of the 2002 Act provides that with leases having an unexpired term in excess of 80 years, there will be no marriage value payable.

6.5   **Intermediate leasehold interests** – Part III of Schedule 6 provides that full compensation must be paid to the owner of any intermediate leasehold interest.

6.6   **Minor intermediate leasehold interests** – Known as "MILIs", these are defined as leases where the reversion has more than 1 month unexpired and the profit rent is less than £5 per annum. In these circumstances the 1993 Act provides that the price payable should be based on the equivalent yield to the Gilt Edge security, 2.5% Consolidated Stock. However, this debenture was redeemed by the Government in July 2015, since when the valuation of MILIs have been determined by reference to the National Loans Fund interest rate.

6.7   **Headleases generally** - In many blocks of flats or converted buildings there is a single lease in respect of the entire building. The owner of that lease will typically be a tenant of the freeholder and in turn the landlord to the various underleases within the building. Usually headleases expire on one of the quarter days (see glossary) and the underleases are granted for a term which typically expires three days earlier. In circumstances where there is this sort of nominal reversion and there is no net rental income, the headlease will have no appreciable value and there is no need to reserve any proportion of the enfranchisement price for the headlessee.

Where there is an appreciable reversion or, where the headlessee has a profit rent (see glossary) then clearly they will be entitled to a fair promotion of the total enfranchisement price and also a due proportion of any marriage value payable.

6.8   **Headleases with negative values** – Where a claim under section 42 is made against a headlessee who has a nominal reversion, and is not therefore the "competent landlord", there are two ways of dealing with the compensation. One way is simply to compensate the headlessee for the loss of the ground rent currently payable by the underlessee. The other way is to agree to commute, or reduce, the head rent by the equivalent amount. If the head rent is not reduced by an equivalent amount, the headlease may acquire a negative value.

If subsequently a claim is made under section 13 to acquire the freehold, the question is whether or not that negative value should be applied to the compensation due to the headlessee. In an Upper Tribunal case heard in 2015 between *Trustees of the Alice Ellen Cooper-Dean Charitable Foundation v Greensleeves Owners Limited* it was held that in these circumstances the headlease would simply have a nil value. It is worth noting that the judge added a comment to say that if this might be considered inappropriate, this was merely what was provided in Schedule 6 and only Parliament could change those provisions. The 2002 Act did not include any amendment to these provisions and the law therefore still applies. This is yet another example of how badly drafted the 1993 Act is.

6.9   **Porter's flat** – There are three potential circumstances relating to the treatment of a porter's flat.

    6.9.1   If the underleases provide for a resident porter and some of the residents have chosen not to participate in the claim those non-participants may insist that the landlord, or their assignee, is bound by that obligation and must maintain a residents' porter. Failure to do so would amount to a derogation of the grant, which is a fundamental tenet of leasehold law. In these circumstances the landlord may not be able to claim an open market value for the porter's flats, as this may be treated as an inalienable right to those non-participating lessees.

    6.9.2   If the leases provide for a resident porter, but there is full participation, the landlord may argue that the claimants will be able to write their own leases once they have acquired the freehold and that will enable them to dispense with the resident porter. In these circumstances the landlord may be able to pursue a claim for vacant possession value but the onus will still lie with the tenants who may argue that it is an essential amenity, without which the flats would have to be devalued.

6.9.3   If the leases do not specifically provide for a resident porter, but merely a porter, even if the porter has actually been resident at the flat for some time, the landlord may succeed in claiming vacant possession value for the flat on the basis that the caretaker could live somewhere else. The tenants may wish to argue that the absence of a resident caretaker would have a deleterious effect on the value of the flats and there will be arguments about the rental value of the existing caretaker's flat and the need to provide alternative accommodation. In most cases the absence of any requirement to maintain a resident caretaker will allow the freeholder to claim vacant possession value.

6.10   **Storage lockers -** The storage lockers are also an amenity and the same considerations as referred to with the porter's flat may apply. It is common for storage lockers to be included in the demise and nearly all modern leases of flats contain a covenant restricting the assignment or sub-letting of part only of the demise. With these circumstances, it would clearly be impossible to realise either a capital sum or a rental income from the lockers and it would therefore be inappropriate to ascribe a separate open market value to them.

6.11   **Optional and mandatory leaseback** – there are two circumstances where a landlord either must, or may choose to, take a leaseback:

6.11.1   Freeholder's mandatory leaseback – Where the freeholder is a housing association and there are leases that do not qualify, that freeholder has the power and must take a leaseback in respect of those non-qualifying leases.

6.11.2   **Freeholder's optional leaseback** – The freeholder is given the right to require 999 year leases at a peppercorn rent to be granted by the enfranchising tenants in certain circumstances, notably:

(a) In respect of any non-qualifying leases, and

(b) Where the freeholder is also a qualifying tenant of a flat.

6.12   **Development** - The landlord can defeat a claim if he is able to prove an intention to carry out a major redevelopment of the property. Such grounds will only be accepted in circumstances where at least two-thirds of the qualifying leases expire within 5 years, and the redevelopment could not reasonably be carried out without gaining vacant possession.

This situation is similar to the provisions relating to business tenancies contained in Section 30(1)d of the Landlord & Tenant Act 1954, where case law has ruled that a landlord must demonstrate that any proposed development is achievable both legally and practically.

6.13   **Completion** – Once the enfranchisement price, the terms of transfer and all other matters set out in section 24(8) have been agreed between the parties, the nominee purchaser company is required to complete the acquisition within two months.

If the matter is not completed within those two months, either party can apply to the court to require the other party to complete. So, unlike the 1967 Act, where a tenant can withdraw their claim at any time, once the terms of transfer have been agreed, this is no longer a unilateral contract and the vendor can pursue the claimant for specific performance.

The application can therefore be made by either party but it cannot be made sooner than two months nor later than four months from the date of agreement. If no application is registered with the court within that period, the claim is considered to be deemed withdrawn.

There is one further aspect which distinguishes these provisions from those contained in the 1967 Act regulations, which is that there is no specific provision for the payment of interest if the purchaser exceeds the initial completion period. However, if the matter is heard by the court, the court would have jurisdiction to award interest at its discretion.

7 Qualification for lease extensions of flats

Chapter II of the 1993 Act provides the framework that enables tenants to serve notice on their landlord to acquire a ninety year extension to their lease. This option was originally intended for tenants of buildings that did not qualify due to the conditions attaching to non-residential elements. It now extends to all qualifying tenants whether their building qualifies or not.

The original Green paper actually proposed an eighty year extension. In 1992 I was advising the Council of Mortgage Lenders in the formation of this legislation and I argued that an eighty year extension was really not sufficient. Surely, I suggested, it would make more sense to enable claimants to acquire a virtual freehold lease of, say, 999 years? My proposal was duly noted and communicated to Parliament. A week later I met again with the Council of Mortgage Lenders and was told that Parliament had taken into account my suggestion and decided to revise this to ninety years. Unfortunately this is just one of many shortcomings in the 1993 Act.

The option of extending a lease rather than acquiring the freehold of a block has proved by far the more popular and perhaps not surprisingly as it does not require the agreement of anybody else in the building and, more relevantly, involves no extra payment in respect of non-participating tenants' leases or other heads of claim.

There is no security of tenure at the end of the extended lease, but the right to acquire a new lease is again available. By continuing to serve notices, a tenant can acquire as long a lease as required, although the costs in purchasing a lease extension on a long lease will more often than not outweigh the marginal gain in value.

7.1   **Criteria for qualification -** In order to qualify for an extended lease a tenant must fulfil the following:

     7.1.0   **Eligible lease** – The same qualification applies as with collective enfranchisement claims defined in paragraph 2.2 above.

     7.1.1   **Eligible tenant** – Section 139 of the 1993 Act has been abolished by Section 130 of the 2002 Act and the need to have resided for 3 out of the last 10 years no longer applies. Instead,

Section 130 provides that the claimant must simply have owned the property for 2 years.

7.1.2   **Time limit if previous claim withdrawn** – If a claim has been made and subsequently withdrawn, a new claim cannot be submitted for at least 12 months. This differs from the rule relating to houses, where the 1967 Act requires that 3 years must have elapsed.

7.2   **Terms of new lease**

The statutory directions are contained in section 57 and provide for the following:

7.2.1   **Term** – The length of the term will be 90 years in excess of the term of the old lease;

7.2.2   **Rent** – No ground rent will be payable throughout;

7.2.3   **Other terms** – The other terms of the new lease will follow the terms of the existing lease, except where certain adjustments are necessary to enable the landlord to continue to manage the building, or where any variation is the subject of an agreement.

7.3   **Procedure to make a claim** - The procedure is considerably easier than with a collective enfranchisement, particularly following the abolition of the residency test.

7.3.1   **Statutory declaration** – This provision has not specifically been abolished but since the residency test has been abolished in favour of 2 years' ownership, there is arguably no need to swear an affidavit. Ownership is clearly a *de facto* matter which can be demonstrated, in the case of registered property, by reference to the Land Registry office copy. Alternatively, it may be deduced from the lease, if the tenant was the original tenant, or by a licence to assign.

7.3.2   **Deposit** – The Leasehold Reform (Collective Enfranchisement & Lease Renewal) Regulations 1993 allow the landlord to serve notice on the tenant to produce a deposit equivalent to £250, or 10% of the amount proposed in the tenant's notice (whichever is the greater) within 14 days of the service of the notice.

7.3.3   **Title** – The landlord is entitled to require the tenant to deduce title within 21 days of service of the claim notice. Such title is usually proved by reference to the office copy entry at the Land Registry.

7.3.4   **Landlord's failure to respond** – The landlord has 2 months in which to oppose or accept the claim. If the landlord fails to respond within this period, the tenant may apply to the court to have the application declared valid on the terms proposed in the notice. Since the terms proposed in the notice tend to be well below a reasonable price, this has given rise to a lot of professional negligence cases where solicitors have failed to serve their counter notice in time

7.3.5   **Landlord's opposition** – If the landlord opposes the claim within the 2 month period, he must, no later than 2 months from date of the counter notice, support this objection by filing an originating application with the court to have the claim declared invalid.

7.3.6   **Application to the FTT** – The claimant lessee must, no sooner than 2 months nor later than 6 months from the date of the Section 45 counter notice, file an application with the First Tier Tribunal (formerly known as the Leasehold Valuation Tribunal), failing which the claim will be deemed to be withdrawn. This is a notorious area for professional negligence and anyone dealing with a Section 42 notice must make very careful diary notes to avoid being out of time.

7.4   **Completion** - The rules are contained in Schedule 2, Section 8 of the Leasehold Reform (Collective and Lease Renewal Regulations) 1993. After the draft lease has been approved, or determined by the court, or deemed to be approved due to either of the parties being out of time to object, either the landlord or the tenant may serve a completion notice. This notice may require completion to take place within 21 days from the date of the completion notice.

If the tenant does not complete by the last allowed date, the landlord may serve a further notice requiring completion to take place within two months, during which time interest will be chargeable on the agreed price at the rate of 2% above the Bank of England Base Rate.

If completion has not taken place in accordance with this second notice, the claim is deemed to be withdrawn. The landlord will then be entitled to deduct from the statutory deposit held all expenses reasonably incurred under section 60 of the 1993 Act.

7.5   **Need to apply to the FTT** – No sooner than two months nor later than six months from the date of the landlord's section 45 counter notice either the tenant or the landlord must make an application to the First Tier Tribunal, failing which the claim will be deemed to be withdrawn. The single most common cause of professional negligence in the world of leasehold enfranchisement is due to solicitors failing to do this. It is perhaps understandable for those who have previously only dealt with 1967 Act claims as there is no equivalent obligation and an application can be made as soon as the claim has been admitted but with some claims it may be several years before it occurs to someone to make an application.

8   Valuation principles applying to lease extensions of flats

The valuation provisions are contained in Schedule 13 to the 1993 Act (as amended). They follow many of the principles established in Section 9(1A) of the Leasehold Reform Act 1967, which was introduced in Section 118 of the Housing Act 1974.

8.1   **Valuation date** – Section 134 of the 2002 Act repealed the provisions in Schedule 13 to the 1993 Act and the valuation date is now the date of claim.

8.2   **Treatment of improvements** - In keeping with Section 9(1A) of the 1967 Act, Schedule 13 provides that tenants' improvements may be disregarded, but there is one important difference. With 1967 Act claims, if the current lease was granted out of the surrender of a previous lease, that previous lease will be linked under Section 3(3) of the 1967 Act. That enables the commencement of the term to begin at the commencement of the previous lease and improvements carried out during the currency of the previous lease can therefore be treated accordingly. However, there is no such provision in the 1993 Act and naturally if, for example, the tenant has built an extension during the qualifying period, although that may be treated as an improvement, it will still be necessary to recognise the potential to create the extension and thus to treat the area as having development value.

8.3   **Loss to the landlord in selling the new lease** – This is the net loss arising from both the deduction of rental income and the fact that the reversion will be postponed for 90 years.

8.4   **Marriage value** – Section 135 of the 2002 Act amends Section 4 of Schedule 13 to the 1993 Act so that, where marriage value applies, it will now be apportioned equally between landlord and tenant. As with valuations for collective enfranchisement and for houses under the 1967 Act, Section 136 of the 2002 Act provides that there shall be no marriage value payable in respect of leases having an unexpired term in excess of 80 years.

8.5   **Headlease with a nominal reversion** – Most headleases expire a few days after the underlease. In these circumstances it begs the question of how the headlessee is able to sell the underlessee a ninety year extension. The answer is that they can't. Accordingly the 1993 Act makes provision for the new lease to be granted by the "competent" landlord, being a landlord with a reversion of more than 90 years. In most instances, therefore, this is the freeholder.

The compensation payable in these circumstances will usually mean the headlessee receiving compensation for the loss of ground rent and the freeholder receiving compensation for the loss of the reversion. Moreover, where the term of the underlease is less than 80 years, the marriage value will also have to be apportioned pro rata these values. However, it has been suggested by one eminent barrister that, in the initial notice, all the marriage value should be allocated to the freeholder and the apportionment should be dealt with afterwards.

8.6   **Headlease with a significant reversion** - Where the reversion is less than 90 years after the expiry of the underlease, the competent landlord will still be the freeholder, but it will be necessary to apportion the value of the reversion between headlessee and freeholder and to apportion the marriage value accordingly.

However, where a headlease expires more than 90 years from the expiry date of the underlease, they can grant the lease extension without reference to the freeholder, subject to the alienation covenant contained in the headlease which may require that the freehold is at least notified.

8.7   **Commuting the head rent** – Where the headlease has a reversion of less than 90 years and is thus unable to grant the statutory lease extension, there is an option. They can either accept compensation for the loss of ground rent or they can, by agreement with the freeholder, waive their right to compensation for the loss of rental income and instead commute (ie reduce) the head rent by the due amount in question. If the headlessee and freeholder do not agree on this strategy, although the headlessee will receive compensation for the loss of income, they will be left with a greater rental liability than they receive and will therefore own a negative interest.

8.8   **Headlessee's right to extend the lease of a single unit** – It is quite common for the owner of a headlease to own one or two flats where no individual underlease has been created. In 2008 two cases, *Howard de Walden Estates Ltd v Aggio* and *Earl Cadogan v 26 Cadogan Square Ltd,* were heard by the House of Lords, who ruled that a headlessee could indeed claim a lease extension on a single flat by virtue of the headlease.

8.9   **Landlord's costs** - Under S.60 the landlord is entitled to recover the reasonable expenses incurred by him and his agents incidental to the claim, including investigation of the right, valuation and conveyancing costs. The costs incurred by him in negotiating the premium are not recoverable save under circumstances where the tenant withdraws. In these circumstances the landlord may be entitled to recover all his costs.

8.10   **Discretionary options** - In some cases the purchase of the statutory lease extension may involve a more expensive investment than is ideally required by the tenant. For example, if a lease, which was originally 99 years, now has 75 years unexpired, it may be that the lessee would be happy merely to restore the lease to its original term. That is a style of negotiation which was quite common before the 1993 Act was introduced. In such circumstances it may be worth approaching the landlord to see if this can be agreed on a voluntary basis.

It certainly should not be assumed that landlords are unwilling to do a deal. In many cases the opportunity to sell a lease extension is exactly what they have been waiting for. However, most landlords are subject to Capital Gains Tax or Corporation Tax and the only way they can avoid having to pay tax is to respond to a statutory claim. This is because the law provides that, when a sale takes place pursuant to a statutory claim, the vendor can claim roll-over relief on any profits received.

Landlords who do not pay tax, such as the Welcome Trust, who are tax exempt due their charitable status, may still not sell on a voluntary basis, but if so that is simply down to their own policy. In some cases a discretionary deal may suit both parties. Even so, it is generally in the lessee's interest to make a formal claim.

8.11   **Advantages of making a formal claim** - First the date of a formal claim is the valuation date, regardless of how long the negotiation may endure. By comparison, with a voluntary negotiation, a landlord can revise the valuation date after a few months if they feel that insufficient progress has been made, during which time the market may have risen and the lease term will certainly have decreased. Secondly, in the event of an impasse, the tenant has the right to refer the matter to a valuation tribunal whereas, with a voluntary negotiation, the landlord could reach a certain point, after which they may say that they are no longer prepared to negotiate.

It might be thought that it will save on costs to deal with this on an informal basis, but that is highly unlikely. Ultimately, by dealing with a claim on a formal basis a tenant will establish what Lord Denning once described as "an equality of bargaining power" and that is worth having.

9 Investment rates

There have been a great many tribunal cases focusing on the appropriate capitalisation and deferment rates applying to 1967 Act and 1993 Act claims. At one time it was normal to select an appropriate yield for the claim in question and to apply one yield to apply to both the term (the capitalisation rate) and the reversion (the deferment rate). Since the Upper Tribunal decision of *Cadogan Estates Limited v Sportelli* (see below) it has been normal to treat these yields separately.

9.1 **Capitalisation rates** – There has been no overriding direction as to the choice of capitalisation rates. From a landlord's perspective, any ground rent is secure in the sense that, if a tenant fails to pay it, that landlord can ultimately apply to forfeit the lease and reclaim the property. However, the courts are extremely reluctant to grant forfeiture and, in reality, most landlords will select a capitalisation rate depending on how easy is it is likely to be to obtain the income and what, if any prospects, are there for growth.

    9.1.1 **No effective ground rent** - Some leases provide that the ground rent shall be an annual payment of a "peppercorn" or perhaps some whimsical notion such as a red rose on midsummer's day. In either case, the lease will invariably provide that such ground rents are only payable "if demanded" and of course the idea of them is that there will be no ground rent payable at all;

    9.1.2 **Nominal ground rents** – A nominal ground rent might be something like £100 pa fixed for the duration of the lease. From an investor's viewpoint, this means zero growth and an amount of money which is not going to justify instructing a solicitor if the tenant is late in paying it. This being the case the investor is going to require a reasonably high yield, at least 6 to 7 per cent above Base Rate.

    9.1.3 **Ground rents subject to predetermined increases** – It is very common to come across leases which provide that the ground rent rises to a predetermined figure during the currency of the lease. In the case of a 125 years lease, this may mean that it doubles every 25 years, or in the case of a 99 year lease, this may mean that it rises every 33 years of the term. In either event, although that is obviously better for a landlord than fixed income, it is still not that exciting. This may typically be reflected in a capitalisation rate which is around 5 - 6 per cent above base rate.

9.1.4   Ground rents geared to a percentage of value – In the mid 1970s it occurred to property managers to provide that a ground rent would rise in value in line with the rise in the market. This could be achieved by providing that the ground rent was subject to a review to a percentage of either rental or capital value. The ground rents geared to a percentage of rental value proved less satisfactory as tenants argued that there was no evidence of a letting for a term of what was typically 25 or 33 years, ie whatever was the period of the review. Ground rents geared to capital value, which could be based on either the vacant freehold value or the value of the property held on its original leasehold term, have proved considerably easier, as it is generally not difficult to find comparable sales evidence to support the revised rent.

9.2   Deferment rates – This is the rate, or yield, needed to determine the present value of the reversion, what used to be referred to in Parry's Valuation Tables as "The present value of £1". At the beginning of this chapter I have referred to *Cadogan Estates Limited v Sportelli*. This was an Upper Tribunal appeal where the tribunal did not just determine the deferment rate in relation to a group of claims that were appealed in one batch, it took the opportunity to prescribe a "generic deferment rate" that was to be employed in all but the most exceptional cases. Whether the Upper Tribunal acted correctly in making this prescription was considered a matter of law and it was referred to the Court of Appeal and eventually to the Supreme Court. The Law Lords ruled that this was entirely within the jurisdiction of the Upper Tribunal, indeed providing guidance to the local tribunals was very much their *raison d'être*.

However the decision was controversial in two respects. First it removed the skill of the valuer in selecting a yield appropriate to the circumstances. Secondly, it proposed that a building in Balham should be valued applying the same deferment rate as a building in Belgravia. This somewhat Procrustean solution has achieved the main objective of reducing the number of applications to the local tribunals, but like all simplified approaches, it is fundamentally flawed.

What *Sportelli* determined is that the deferment rate for houses should be 4.75% and that the deferment rate for flats, due to the management issues, should be one quarter per cent higher at 5.00%. The only exceptions envisaged were where a building was suffering from obsolescence or the unexpired term of the lease was significantly longer than 80 years or shorter than 20 years

9.3   **Bases for departing from Sportelli** – The First Tier Tribunals are bound by directions handed down by the Upper Tribunal (Lands Chamber) and that includes following the principles established in *Cadogan Estates Limited v Sportelli*. However those principles did leave some room for discretion, particularly with very long and very short leases. Also there may be discretion where a property is shown to have less favourable growth prospects, or it may be affected by obsolescence, or there may be management difficulties. For those wishing to investigate this further the following authorities have departed from the generic deferment rate defined in Sportelli and, although some of these decisions have since been criticised as illogical, it may be worth considering the arguments that were accepted;

        9.3.1   *Nell Gwynn House Freehold Ltd v NGH Properties Ltd (2008)* – where it was stated that deferment rates should be higher for leases having more than 75 years;

        9.3.2   *Polydorou (Antonius) v Management Nominees (Reversions) Ltd* - relating to a building affected by obsolescence in South Kensington;

        9.3.3   *Zuckerman v Calthorpe Estates Trustees* (2009) - where a block in Birmingham was held to have reduced growth prospects;

        9.3.4   *Ashdown Hove Ltd v Remstar Properties Ltd* (2010) - relating to a building in Hove, East Sussex where a higher yield was accepted due both to obsolescence and the term of the leases, being 125 years;

        9.3.5   *Cadogan Properties Ltd v Earl Cadogan* (2010) – where it was accepted that leases in Cadogan Square, Knightsbridge, should be valued at a deferment rate in excess of 5.00% due to the unexpired terms being less than 20 years.

9.4   **Dual rates of interest** – Dual rates are traditionally employed in valuing the income payable to a leaseholder. The idea is that a lease is a wasting asset and therefore, to put a leaseholder on the same footing as a freeholder, it is necessary to apply, in addition to the remunerative rate, an accumulative rate designed to replace capital in the way that a sinking fund operates. In addition, as a lease is a less attractive form of investment than a freehold, it is usual to apply a slightly higher remunerative rate than that which would be applied to a freehold investment. So, for example, an income which is valued at a freehold remunerative rate of 5.5% might, if the interest were leasehold, be valued at a remunerative rate of 6.50% and this would be combined with an accumulative rate of perhaps 2.00%. The accumulative rate is intended to represent guaranteed income after tax and is thus extremely cautious.

In the 1970s and 1980s it was common to make a tax allowance for the accumulative rate of interest, so that, for example, an income might be valued at a rate of 6.5% and 2.0% (assuming tax at 30% or 40%). The tax adjustment does not actually make a significant amount of difference and this practice has largely been disbanded.

10   Leasehold to freehold relativity and related issues

10.1   **The "No Act World"** - Both the 1967 Act and 1993 Act make a leasehold property more saleable, and ultimately more valuable, than it otherwise would be. A lease with, say, thirty years unexpired would today be of little interest to most purchasers if they could not extend that lease as a matter of right, or expect to be able to extend that lease on a voluntary basis, as used to happen before the statutory provisions were introduced.

It is recognised that, where these statutory provisions apply, the leasehold property in question is likely to be more valuable than it would be if they did not apply. This is due largely to the marriage value provision contained in both the 1967 and 1993 Acts which provide that, where there is marriage value, the lessee is only required to pay 50% of that value. Moreover, if the unexpired term is more than 80 years, even if it can be shown that there is marriage value, in the context of a statutory claim, the lessee is not required to pay part of that marriage value.

Marriage value is an often misunderstood term. It simply means profit and it exists because the sum of the current leasehold and freehold interests is usually less than the vacant freehold value. So it is calculated by deducting from the vacant freehold value the current leasehold and freehold interests, but that's where it gets tricky.

In order to avoid double counting and to arrive at a true profit, it is necessary to value both the current leasehold and freehold interests excluding any marginal value attributable to the Act (whichever Act applies). In the case of the freeholder, it means excluding any extra amount that a purchaser of that interest might pay in anticipation of receiving some marriage value when the tenant makes a claim. In the case of the tenant, it means excluding any extra amount that a purchaser might reasonably pay in the knowledge that they could make a claim.

This principle used to be known as valuing the interests "excluding prospects of marriage" but more recently, and in reference to a later tribunal decision, it has become known as valuing the interests in the "No Act World".

10.2   **Relative value by reference to graphs** – The most popular way of valuing the leasehold interest in the "No Act World" is to say that any length of lease can be valued as a percentage, or "relativity", of vacant freehold value. This is because virtually all residential property is now protected by either the 1967 Act or 1993 Act and there is therefore no market evidence to show what, for example, a thirty year lease, would sell for if it were outside this protection.

In Arrowdell Ltd v Coniston Court (North) Hove Ltd the Upper Tribunal commented: "We have been acutely aware of the difficulty of reaching a satisfactory conclusion on relativity in the light of the inadequacy of the available evidence, and it is clear that this is a problem that is liable to confront LVTs in all such cases. The likelihood is that decisions will be varied and inconsistent, while if local perceptions of relativities are built up as the result of decisions and settlements it is improbable that these will properly reflect no-Act values. Against this background we consider that graphs of relativity are capable of providing the most useful guidance."

There is a website referred to as the "Graph of Graphs" which allows the user to select an unexpired term and it will show the average percentage value deriving from around eight of the most respected graphs, including my own. It also shows graphs based on tribunal decisions.

The tribunals have made it clear that evidence of comparable properties sold in the market will always be regarded as the best evidence. However, the Upper Tribunal (Lands Chamber) has directed on more than seven occasions in the last ten years that where there are no properties that can be considered "good comparables", graphs of relativity are recommended as a useful reference.   The First Tier Tribunals have not always followed this advice, which is disappointing because, apart from resolving appeals, the main purpose of the Upper Tribunal is to establish guidelines that these local tribunals should follow. This was made abundantly clear by the Supreme Court in the *Sportelli* case.

10.3   **Relative value by recognising a percentage uplift** - Another method which tribunals have been keen to encourage is to look at the open market value of a leasehold property and to recognise that a percentage of that value must be attributable to the Act. This sounds logical except that it is almost invariably going to involve more guesswork than applying an established schedule of relativities. In general, the longer a lease is, the less effect the Act is likely to have on the value of that lease. So, whereas the value of a lease with 65 years unexpired may be considered to be 5% more valuable as a consequence of these statutory rights, a lease with 25 years unexpired may be considered to be 20% more valuable as a consequence of these rights. In other words, with a 65 year lease, you might deduct 5% from the market value to arrive at the correct statutory value, but with a lease of 25 years, you might deduct 20%.

10.4   **Varying ground rent obligations** – It is important to bear in mind that it is not just the unexpired term of a lease that determines its relative value. Ground rents can vary enormously and have a significant effect on the relative value of a lease. Some leases provide for the annual payment of a peppercorn, whereas others are geared to a percentage of freehold or rental value and reviewable throughout the term of the lease. One Leasehold Valuation Tribunal decision (as the First Tier Tribunal was then known) introduced a system which has been fairly widely adopted. This case, *Millard Investments Ltd v Cadogan Estates Ltd LON/LVT 2005*, was determined on the basis that a ground rent not exceeding 0.1% of the equivalent vacant freehold value would not affect the relative value of the leasehold, but any amount in excess of this should be reflected in a pro rata deduction from the relative value of the leasehold.

10.5   **Relativity in different locations** - Whether one values an existing lease by reference to a graph of relativities or by reference to its open market value with an appropriate adjustment there is always the question of whether such percentages should apply universally or whether they should vary from location to location. For example, a house in the suburbs offered on the market with an unexpired lease of 25 years and without the benefit of the Act may be almost unsaleable. It will certainly be unmortgageable. On the other hand, a house in Belgravia offered on the market with the same length lease may be perfectly saleable, as there is no shortage of cash purchasers. The logical inference to be drawn from this is that a house in Prime Central London should be valued at a higher relative value than one located in the suburbs, where a sale may be largely dependent on the ability to extend the lease. This issue was referred to a local valuation tribunal, *Spencer v Bindra*, where it was determined that relativity is not location sensitive. This may have been determined in order to encourage some consistency, applying the sort of thinking that led to the ''generic'' deferment rate introduced in *Cadogan Estates Limited v Sportelli*. Unfortunately this is yet another example of the tribunals putting simplicity above equity.

10.6 **Effect on relativity of other onerous covenants** – In 2015 an appeal was heard at the Upper Tribunal between *Roberts and Thain v Fernandez* involving a lease with a very unusual covenant. It allowed the landlord to charge the tenant 1% of the sale price every time the lease was sold. The landlord argued that this made the lease less valuable and that this should therefore give rise to a lower relative value. The tribunal dismissed this on the basis that, in accordance with section 57, the new lease would have to contain the same covenant as the old lease. The point simply is that the only thing that changes with these lease extensions is the term of the lease, which is extended by ninety years and the ground rent, which is extinguished. Accordingly, however onerous the existing lease may be, it will not have any effect on the relative value of the existing term.

10.7 **Tenant's need to propose a sensible price** - The 1993 Act requires both those making a claim under Section 13 (a collective enfranchisement) and those making a claim under Section 42 (an individual claim for a ninety year lease extension) to propose a price.

The original provisions of the 1993 Act require claimants to instruct a professional valuer to undertake a valuation of the landlord's interest before they could serve notice. The purpose of this slightly patronising requirement was presumably to ensure that the claimant would know what they were letting themselves in for. This was particularly relevant given that they would be liable for the landlord's legal and valuation costs if they later discovered that it was all rather more expensive than they had imagined and had to withdraw their claim.

This requirement to obtain professional advice was withdrawn under the 2002 Act, but the question still remained as to what was intended by the obligation to propose a price at all. The 1967 Act, after all, merely requires the tenant to apply to buy the freehold (or a fifty year extension). There is no requirement to propose a price. The following case precedents have sought to clarify things:

10.7.1 *Cadogan v Morris (1999)* – the tenant in this case had proposed something like £10 in circumstances where the realistic price was well over £100,000. The County Court initially found in favour of the tenant on the basis that, although it was obviously a cheeky proposal, it did not invalidate the claim. The Court of Appeal, however, took the view that there was an implicit obligation to propose a sensible amount and the tenant had clearly proposed a silly amount. The question then arose as to how a lawyer could know whether an amount proposed was silly or not. The judge suggested that a silly amount was like an elephant, difficult to describe but you knew one when you saw one.

10.7.2 *Mount Cook Land Ltd v Rosen (2002)* – the judge in this case tried to be a bit more helpful by saying that the price should be based on evidence; and

10.7.3 *Westbrook Dolphin Square Ltd v Friends Provident Life and Pensions Ltd (2011) – which, while not actually rubbishing Mount Cook, said that the amount proposed "does not necessarily have to be within a valuation range or a price which the tenant believed would be or even might be accepted....and which no reasonable landlord would have dismissed as patently absurd or nonsensical, even if it was unlikely to be accepted."*

10.8 **Landlord's need to propose a sensible price** – The landlord is not required by law to propose a sensible price.

10.9 **Why it is only the tenant who has to propose a sensible price** - It may seem inequitable, or at least inconsistent, that it is only the tenant who has to propose a sensible price. The reason for this is probably to do with the consequences of that initial proposal. It will be obvious that there will always be a margin between a buyer's price and a seller's price, the former being represented by the tenant's proposal and the latter being represented by the landlord's counter proposal.

The tenant's initial notice will state the deadline by which the landlord must either accept the claim or serve a counter notice, usually admitting the claim but not the price proposed. However, if the landlord is out of time in serving his counter notice, he is obliged to accept the price proposed by the tenant and, notwithstanding the judicial directives referred to in 10.7 above, that price may be very significantly less than the correct price.

On the other hand, if the landlord proposes in his counter notice a price which is significantly higher than it should be, that cannot disadvantage the tenant who can then enter into negotiations to agree the correct price. The only thing to bear in mind is that, if the tenant has accepted a contingency fee basis based on the reduction from the landlord's quoting price and the landlord proposes a totally unreasonable price, it would be appropriate for the client to require his valuer to revise the fee basis before taking the matter any further.

10.10   **The "Escalator Clause" in Grosvenor leases** – This is something which Grosvenor created as a tax benefit and it applies to some leases in Belgravia between the Duke of Westminster and Grosvenor Estates (Belgravia) Limited. It involved a system whereby, after 42 years of a 200 year term which started in March 1984, Grosvenor Estates Belgravia would pay over to the Duke of Westminster their earnings on a sliding scale. Initially 5% was payable but this would rise by 5% every year until after 59 years they would pay 90% of all earnings.

A claim was made for a house in Chester Street, Belgravia, where this arrangement was in place. It was heard by the Upper Tribunal in the case of *Grosvenor Estate Belgravia v Klaasmeyer* in 2006. The tribunal decided that the best way to treat this was to discount the value of the reversion by 30%. Some felt this would have been better dealt with by an adjustment of the yield, but in keeping with so many recent decisions, the tribunal went for an easy option and the authority still stands.

11   Disputes

Whether the matter is an enfranchisement claim under the 1967 Act, the determination of a Section 15 rent, a collective claim under the 1993 Act or an individual lease extension there are two areas which may be the subject of dispute. These are:

11.1   **Points of law** - The tribunals have very limited jurisdiction on points of law which are therefore referral in the first instance to the County Court. If there is an appeal it will usually be heard at either the Chancery Division or the Queen's Bench Division. It is quite surprising how many cases relating to leasehold enfranchisement have ended up not just at the Court of Appeal, but on further appeal to the House of Lords, which at the behest of Tony Blair became known as the Supreme Court.

11.2   **Valuation issues** – There are two aspects to this – the price payable for the interest to be acquired and the landlord's costs in responding to the claim, for which the tenant is responsible.

        11.2.1   **First Tier Tribunals** – In the first instance the determination of the price is referred to a local valuation tribunal known as the First Tier Tribunal (formerly known as the Leasehold Valuation Tribunal). Such references are fairly informal. There is no need to appoint counsel, although the parties usually do, and evidence is not given on oath.

        11.2.2   **Costs** - Costs are usually resolved without a problem, but if there is a dispute, the same local tribunals have the power under Section 91 of the 1993 Act to tax the landlord's costs without the need to refer the matter to a Taxing Master of the High Court. (See Section on Costs at 12.0 below)

11.3   **Upper Tribunal (Lands Chamber)** – The Upper Tribunal hears appeals from the First Tier Tribunal. They are not strictly speaking appeals in that the parties are free to introduce fresh evidence and the submissions made during the LVT hearing are treated as no more than a matter of record.

11.4   **Right to appeal** - Either party can appeal within 2 months of the award being given by the First Tier Tribunal, but there is no absolute right to an appeal. As with the law courts, the FTT has to agree to the appeal although, if the FTT is not prepared to agree, the litigant can apply to the Upper Tribunal for the right to appeal and it is not uncommon for the Upper Tribunal to overturn the decision of the FTT in this respect.

11.5   **Further rights of appeal** – The Upper Tribunal has the final say on any point of valuation. If there are any unresolved points of law, it may be possible to lodge an appeal with the Court of Appeal and of course any decision of the Court of Appeal may in turn be referred to the Supreme Court.

11.6   **Whether interest can be charged from the date of claim** – In 1999 in *Kamara & Ezekiel v Elghanian* a question arose as to whether the Upper Tribunal (Lands Chamber) - then simply known as the Lands Tribunal - could and, if they could, whether they would, award interest on the enfranchisement price from the date of claim. The subject claim was unusual in that the tenants had served their notice some seven years earlier, but the matter had been delayed due to the need to clear probate. The landlords claimed that the tenants had deliberately prolonged the procedure and had benefited in the meantime by letting the house.

Section 19(A) of the Arbitration Act 1950 provides in Rule 32 the powers that the Upper Tribunal has in relation to awarding costs. These were revised in Schedule I, Part IV of the Administration of Justice Act 1982 and further revised in 1996 by Statutory Instrument No. 1022. The position now is that the Upper Tribunal is empowered both to award costs at its discretion and, since SI. 1022, they can also award interest.

However, in *Kamara* the President of the Upper Tribunal considered that it would be inappropriate to award interest for the basic reason that interest can only be chargeable once an amount has been determined and until the Lands Tribunal had determined the figure, that amount was not known.

The corollary to this is for landlords to file an application at the earliest opportunity which, in the case of a 1967 Act claim, is any time after the claim has been admitted.   In the case of a 1993 Act claim it is a four month window beginning no sooner than two months after the claim has been admitted and no later than six months after it has been admitted.

12   Costs

With all statutory claims the law is intended to provide that the person being served with a claim should be entitled to recover the costs that they will incur in responding to the claim. The claim is not after all their idea and it is analogous to somebody being entitled to claim costs against a local authority making a compulsory purchase.

Costs tend to divide between legal and valuation costs and they are payable once a statutory notice has been served, whether the claim proceeds or not, which is at least one reason why it makes sense to obtain professional valuation advice before serving a notice.

Although the 1967 Act and the 1993 Act are drafted slightly differently, the aim of the legislation in both cases is that costs must be mitigated. Accordingly, if a claim is withdrawn, costs can be recovered only to the extent that they have actually been incurred.

12.1   **The 1967 Act** – Costs are recoverable under section 9(4) of the Act and provide for the following:

(a)   *any investigation by the landlord of that person's right to acquire the freehold;*

(b)   *any conveyance or assurance of the house and premises or any part thereof or of any outstanding estate or interest therein;*

(c)   *deducing, evidencing and verifying the title to the house and premises or any estate or interest therein;*

(d)   *making out and furnishing such abstracts and copies as the person giving the notice may require;*

(e)   *any valuation of the house and premises;*

12.2   **The 1993 Act for collective enfranchisement claims** – Costs are recoverable under section 33 for the following:

(a)   *any investigation reasonably undertaken of the question*

> *whether any interest in the specified premises or other property is liable to acquisition in pursuance of the initial notice, or of any other question arising out of that notice;*

(b)   *deducing, evidencing and verifying the title to any such interest;*

(c)   *making out and furnishing such abstracts and copies as the nominee purchase may require;*

(d)   *any valuation of any interest in the specified premises or other property;*

(e)   *any conveyance of any such interest;*

12.3   **The 1993 Act for individual lease extensions** – Costs relating to a claim served under section 60 are recoverable for the following:

(a)   *any investigation reasonably undertaken of the tenant's right to a new lease*

(b)   *any valuation of the tenant's flat obtained for the purpose of fixing the premium or any other amount payable by virtue of Schedule 13 in connection with the grant of a new lease under section 56*

(c)   *the grant of a new lease under that section;*

12.4   **The extent to which costs must be reasonable -** It is axiomatic that any legal obligation to pay costs should be subject to a test of reasonableness. In this respect, there is an interesting provision in Section 33 of the 1993 Act which states, in relation to collective enfranchisement claims, that such costs: *"shall only be regarded as reasonable if and to the extent that costs in respect of such services might reasonably be expected to have been incurred by him if the circumstances had been such that he was personally liable for all such costs".*

It is not entirely clear, but seems reasonable, that this test of reasonableness would equally apply to costs claimed under section 60 of the 1993 Act (individual lease extensions) and Section 9(4) of the 1967 Act.

13   Right-to-buy provisions

Much of this guide is devoted to an explanation of the legislation that enables tenants to serve notice on their landlords either to extend their lease or to acquire their freehold. However, there is another way in which tenants may collectively purchase the freehold interest in their property. This arises where the freeholder wishes to sell to a third party. Under the provisions of the Landlord & Tenant Act 1987, the tenants may be able to exercise a statutory right to buy the freehold of their block at the price which their landlord is proposing to accept from a third party.

For many years the 1987 Act was a largely toothless piece of legislation, principally as there were no penalties available to punish landlords who did not comply with its requirements. These were brought to light in *Mainwaring v. Henry Smith's Charities Trustees (Court of Appeal 1996),* which gave rise to some important amendments as regards procedure which now are contained in S.89-93 of the Housing Act 1996. These provide that landlords who do not comply with the procedure may face criminal proceedings.

For tenants given the opportunity, purchasing the freehold under these circumstances may mean that will do better than they would under the 1993 Act. The reason for this is that although the price may well contain "hope value" – see glossary – it will not contain 50% of the marriage value which is what they would be required to pay if they initiated the transfer with a claim made under the 1993 Act.

13.1   **Qualification** - The criteria required to be a qualifying tenant are not as rigorous as that required to serve notice under the 1967 Act or the 1993 Act. Most tenancies qualify, even those residential leases held in company names. However, there are some exceptions:

         3.1.1   **Non-qualifying tenancies** – The following tenancies will not be deemed to qualify:

                 a) Assured Tenancies as defined by the Housing Act 1980;

                 b) Business tenancies (this does not exclude residential tenancies where the lease is in the name of a company); and

                 c) Service tenancies.

13.1.2   **Non-qualifying tenants** – There are some circumstances where a tenancy may qualify, but where the tenant himself is unable to qualify. These are where the tenant is:

a) An owner of more than 1 flat in the building; or

b) The owner of a flat and any part of the common   parts.

13.2   Circumstances where the landlord is not under an obligation

13.2.1   The landlord is not obliged to offer the property to the tenants in circumstances where there is an insufficient number of qualifying tenants in the building. Such circumstances are when:

13.2.2   The building has less than 2 flats held by qualifying tenants;

13.2.3   50% or less of the total number of flats in the building are held by non-qualifying tenants.

13.2.4   In addition to the above, there are certain landlords who are exempt from the provisions of the Act. These include resident landlords, local authorities, development corporations, housing associations, housing action trusts and charitable housing trusts.

13.3   **Procedure a landlord is required to observe** – The landlord is obliged to serve a Section 5 notice on at least 90% of the qualifying tenants in the building. If there are less than 10 qualifying tenants, therefore, they must serve the notice on all of them. The notice must specify the price at which the tenants are invited to purchase his interest, and also specify a period of not less than 2 months from the date of service of the notice by which the tenants must respond.

At least 50% of the qualifying tenants must respond to the notice by the time specified if they wish to continue with the procedure. In circumstances where the landlord has not agreed a price with a prospective purchaser, but wishes to sell his interest by public auction, he must serve a Section 5 notice inviting the tenants to match the bid raised at public auction. The notice must be served at least 4 months, and not more than 6 months before the auction date.

13.4   **Nominee purchaser** – Within 2 months of responding to the Section 5 notice above, the tenants must advise the landlord of their nominated purchaser. The vehicle for such a purchase would normally be in the form of a limited company in which the tenants would own shares, and from which they would be able to grant themselves leases and manage the building.

In the event that the property is to be sold by public auction, the tenants still have 2 months in which to respond to the Section 5 notice, but they then have only 28 days to nominate their purchaser.

13.5   **Contract for sale** – The landlord must send out a contract for sale within 1 month of receipt of the information on the nominated purchaser above. In the event that the property has been disposed at auction, and the tenants have offered to match the bid, the landlord must send out a copy of the contract to the nominated purchaser within 7 days of the auction.

13.6   **Signing of contract and exchange** – Within 2 months of receiving the contract of sale from the landlord, the nominee purchaser must sign and pay a deposit. The contracts must be then exchanged within 7 days from that date.

13.7   **Withdrawal from the procedure** - Should at any time the tenants or nominee purchaser decide to withdraw from the procedure, there may be a liability to meet the landlord's costs up to that point. The rules governing the liability for costs contained in Section 9 and 14 of the 1987 Act are highly complex providing different rules according to how far the claim has progressed and the circumstances under which the tenants have withdrawn.

13.8   **Section 18 notice** - This is a notice that may be served by the prospective purchaser on the tenants, which will enable him to enquire as to whether they have been served Section 5 notices by the landlord, and if not, whether they wish to be served with them.

For many years it was standard practice for landlords to ignore the requirements of Section 5 and to rely on the purchaser to satisfy the statutory obligations by serving a Section 18 notice. This is because the time period from the date of service of a Section 18 notice that tenants have to protect their position is 28 days, rather than the 2 months under a Section 5 notice. If the tenants fail to respond with the necessary majority in time, then the landlord will not be obliged to serve Section 5 notices and the sale can proceed.

Under Section 91 of the Housing Act 1996 it is now a criminal offence for a landlord to sell his interest without first serving Section 5 notices. Accordingly, the days of frustrating the Act by service of a Section 18 notice, in the hope that the limited time available to tenants would prevent them from securing their rights, are over.

13.9   **Compulsory acquisition** - Part III of the 1987 Act gives qualifying tenants the right to serve a compulsory purchase notice on their landlord to buy his interest. The 1993 Act and the Housing Act 1996 extends the existing conditions, both in terms of the definition of a qualifying tenant and the circumstances under which a notice can be served.

This will not necessarily be an alternative to enfranchising as the qualifying tenants can only buy their landlord's interest and the landlord may not be the freeholder. However, whether the immediate landlord is a freeholder or not, by acquiring that interest, the occupational tenants may be able to establish management control and this may be more important than extending the terms of the existing leases. However, Part II, Chapter I of the 2002 Act allows a group of tenants to acquire management control simply by demonstrating that they would fulfil the criteria for collective enfranchisement. Although this provision does not necessarily get rid of a landlord, it may in many circumstances be the best solution.

14   Commonhold

There is not a lot to say about Commonhold. In July 1996 the Lord Chancellor's Department published the Government's Commonhold Bill. It took until 1ˢᵗ May, 2002 before Commonhold became law under the Commonhold and Leasehold Reform Act 2002 and what a damp squib it has proved to be.

The idea of commonhold was to offer a new and exciting form of property tenure for owners of flats and maisonettes. English lawyers have long taken the view that it is inefficient to sell flats as freeholds (known as "flying freeholds") as it can be difficult to enforce covenants essential to the upkeep of a building. Equally it has long been considered that the leasehold system is archaic.

Commonhold is a freehold development divided into separately owned individual parts with arrangements for communal management and shared ownership of common parts through the medium of a "commonhold association".

The individual flats or other properties that are comprised in a commonhold are referred to in the Act as "units". A person who owns a unit will own the freehold estate in that unit. Consequently, there will be no other person (such as a landlord) who will have the ownership rights superior to those of the unit owner. The right of a unit owner to retain his unit will be indefinite. Unlike a leasehold interest, ownership of a commonhold will not be limited by reference to a particular period of time.

A unit owner will have certain statutory rights and obligations in relation to his fellow unit owners and the commonhold association, which will be responsible for the management of the commonhold as a whole. These rights and obligations are intended to ensure that the units are properly maintained and that they are not used in ways which would be detrimental to the rights of the occupiers of other units in the commonhold.

There is no direct entry to commonhold. A group of lessees in a block will still have to enfranchise under Part I of the 1993 Act. Once that process is completed, they may then elect to form a Commonhold rather than the usual arrangement of a limited company to act as the freeholder with each participating lessee being both a shareholder of that company and the owner of a virtual freehold lease.

It is a system which is almost entirely logical. Unfortunately this is England and we tend to be a little suspicious of such things. This is, after all, the country that likes to adhere to tradition, however maladroit that tradition may be. The fact that many English people, let alone foreigners, find the current system quite incomprehensible is not of itself a cause for concern. After all, some people do not even understand cricket.

As a result, Commonhold has been an unprecedented failure. So far, no more than about twenty commonholds have been created in the whole country with most solicitors wanting nothing to do with it. "Better the devil you know" we like to say, and so the leasehold system continues.

15   Glossary

These are some of the terms frequently used in relation to residential property and leasehold enfranchisement in particular. There are many more terms used to describe the physical structure of buildings which are outside the scope of this guide and are not therefore covered in this list.

Adverse differential – This is where, in a Section 9(1) valuation, the yield applied to the Section 15 rent is different to the deferment rate. Lord Denning MR observed in *Official Custodian for Charities & others v Goldridge* (1973) that it would not make sense to decapitalise at one rate and recapitalise at a different rate.

Alienation covenant – This is the generic term for a covenant in a lease which deals with such matters as assignment, sub-letting and sharing possession. Most leases require the tenant to obtain the landlord's licence to assign. There are some fairly rare leases, such as those in the Inns of Court, which are not residential leases in any event, where there are absolute restrictions on assignment. Otherwise, where a covenant in a lease provides that any defined alienation will require the consent of the landlord, such consent cannot unreasonably be withheld under Section 19(1) of the Landlord and Tenant Act 1927.

Appurtenance – A minor right, interest or privilege which passes when the title to the principal property is transferred.

Assignment – A lease is a bilateral contract between two parties, whose interests cannot exist in isolation and cannot be sold as though they did. A sale of a lease is therefore treated as an assignment, although since the Landlord and Tenant (Covenants) Act 1995 came into force, the distinction is less significant.

Assured Periodic Tenancy – This is a tenancy pursuant to Part I of the Housing Act 1988. Since 15 January 1999 owners of qualifying residential leases have no longer had the right to claim a tenancy under the Rent Act 1977, which involves paying a "fair rent". Instead, under Section 186 and Schedule 10 to the Local Government and Housing Act 1989, they may claim an Assured Periodic tenancy, which provides the same security of tenure, but requires them to pay a rent based on the open market rental value of their property.

Clarise deduction – This is a deduction to reflect a tenant's right to hold over in a Section 9(1) valuation. See section 3.15 which deals with a tenant's right to hold over.

Clear lease – One where the landlord has no actual or contingent liability for outgoings of any kind and the rent is effectively a net income before tax.

Commonhold – A form of property tenure introduced by the Commonhold and Leasehold Reform Act 2002. The unit owner has a perpetual interest in the Commonhold Association and is thus in a position analogous to the owner of a freehold house, except of course that there are rights and obligations attaching to that Commonhold designed to ensure the building is well maintained. It took more than 12 years in the Lord Chancellor's Office to come up with these provisions and they have been extraordinarily unsuccessful with only a handful of commonholds having been created since this legislation was introduced.

Community Charge – A Local Government tax that replaced rateable values for residential property in 1990 until it was replaced by the Council Tax (see below).

Competent landlord – The competent landlord is the person or company who is in a position to grant lease extensions to anyone eligible to serve a notice under s.42 of the LRHUDA. In most cases it will of course be the freeholder. However, it may be an intermediate lessee, providing they have a reversion that expires more than 90 years after the underlease in question. In situations where the freehold of a block of flats has been acquired by a majority of the lessees and there are some lessees who did not participate, the competent landlord will either be the new freehold company or, if the enfranchisement was facilitated by the involvement of a "white knight investor" (see definition below) then that white knight investor will be the competent landlord to those remaining lessees.

Copyhold – An obsolete form of property tenure enforceable only by the lord of the manor.

Counsel – This is the term usually applied to barristers as, for example: "obtaining counsel's opinion" and "appointing counsel", not to be confused with a council which is a local authority. See also QC below.

Council Tax – The form of Local Government taxation that replaced the Community Charge or "Poll Tax" as a means of raising revenue from residential property. It is based on a combination of the value of the property, placing it into one of several set categories of value, with adjustments to the amount demanded according to the number of occupiers.

Covenant – A term or obligation in a lease.

Curtilage – An area of land attaching to a building. This crops up in collective enfranchisement claims and in practice is a rather ill-defined term which has given rise to several legal disputes.

Deducing title – Following any enfranchisement claim a landlord may, amongst other things, require the tenant to deduce title. This means to prove ownership. It is generally achieved by producing the Land Registry Office copy entry (see Land Registry). This can be obtained online or over the counter at 32 Lincoln's Inn Fields, London WC2.

Delaforce effect – Deriving from *Delaforce v Evans* (1970), this is an argument that evidence deriving from a settlement may be prejudiced by the tendency of a tenant to be less inclined to incur the costs of referring the matter to a tribunal than a landlord would. This is based on the assumption that a landlord might have greater resources to cover the costs of litigation and might also be motivated to incur further costs as the decision might have a knock-on effect for any other properties they might own. The corollary to this is that a tenant may have paid more than they should and the evidence deriving from such a settlement should be regarded as unreliable. There is, however, a corresponding landlord's argument that they are the ones who are losing out due to the delay in reaching a settlement and accordingly they are more likely to have capitulated than the tenant. It is inevitably a somewhat circular argument and the case is generally regarded now as something of an old chestnut.

Dilapidations - This is straightforward English and does not have any special meaning, but it is particularly germane to long residential leases, which invariably contain an obligation to maintain the property in good order. Accordingly, if it should come to the attention of a landlord that a lessee is in breach of their repairing obligations, that landlord may draw up a schedule of dilapidations. This will detail the works which the lessee may be required to carry out and failure to do so may ultimately allow the landlord to forfeit the lease. Equally, if a lease is left to expire, there may be dilapidation liabilities at that time.

Enfranchise – Literally to set free. In property terminology this refers to the statutory right of a leaseholder to buy his freeholder's interest. It is often used to refer to the right under Chapter Ii of the 1993 Act to acquire a lease extension. This is not really enfranchisement as the claimant will still be a lessee and, although they will have done a great deal to protect their investment, they will still be subject to the same terms and conditions as they were under the old lease.

Entirety value – This phrase derives from Section 9(1) of the 1967 Act and is intended to mean the most valuable building that could reasonably be expected to be built on a site.

Escalator clause – This is a reference to a clause created by the lawyers acting for the Grosvenor Estate, who created a headlease between the Duke of Westminster and a part of the Grosvenor Estate referred to as Grosvenor Estates Belgravia. The effect of this was considered in 2006 by the Upper Tribunal in *Grosvenor Estate Belgravia v Klaasmeyer* where it was determined that it would have a significant effect on the value of the reversion of the headlease.

Escheat – The process by which a property may revert to the Crown if it is owned by a person who dies without legal heirs.

Estate Management Scheme – An EMS is a device enabling a disenfranchised landlord, who continues to own neighbouring properties, to retain some management control on the enfranchised property. They were first established by Section 19 of the Leasehold Reform Act 1967 and required a High Court Order to be implemented. Chapter IV of the 1993 Act amended those provisions by giving the Leasehold Valuation Tribunals (now the First Tier Tribunals) the power to implement them. Since this time there have been several new ones. They are often met with some degree of protest, particularly from those who, having enfranchised, may feel that they have just bought an unencumbered freehold. An EMS looks similar to a lease, containing clauses dealing with repair, maintenance and alterations. In practice, they amount to little more restriction than a local authority Conservation Area.

Fair rent – The rent determined by the Rent Officer Service in accordance with the provisions of the Rent Act 1977. This basis is different from open market rental value as it is based on the principle of ignoring scarcity in the market.

First Tier Tribunals – These are local tribunals, previously known as Leasehold Valuation Tribunals, which hear applications to determine claims under the 1967 and 1993 Acts as well as matters relating to service charges and applications for the right to manage a block of flats under the 2002 Act.

Fixed rent – This is a rent which is set to remain the same throughout the term of the lease.

Freehold – Defined in law as a *"tenure in fee simple absolute in possession"*, it is the highest form of property tenure offered in English law.

Flying freehold – An expression applied to a property which is not vertically divided (e.g. a flat or maisonette) which is held as an independent freehold. Such properties are extremely rare and generally considered unsatisfactory by mortgage lenders due to the difficulty of enforcing covenants.

Geared rent – This is a rent which is subject to periodic reviews "geared" to a percentage of either rental or capital value. These may be distinguished from ground rents which are subject to predetermined increases and do not therefore need to be reviewed.

Generic deferment rate - This phrase derives from an Upper Tribunal Case of *Cadogan v Sportelli* which prescribed a yield or rate to apply to the valuation of residential reversions. The question of whether the Upper Tribunal had the authority to make such a prescription was referred to the Supreme Court who ruled that it did.

GIA – This stands for Gross Internal Area. Residential property is normally measured according to its gross internal area, which is basically the entire area of the property including corridors, staircases and ancillary rooms. Only where there is limited headroom is floor space excluded or distinguished. This differentiates it from commercial property, which is generally referred to according to its "net lettable area".

Ground rent – Originally an amount of rent representing the open market rental value of the ground or site. Today it is an arbitrary amount of money generally chosen by the landlord with the view to achieving as much income as possible without affecting the price achievable for the sale of the lease. It is also a factor to be taken into account in determining qualification for various valuation bases under the 1967 Act.

Headlessee – A tenant whose landlord is the freeholder and who is a landlord himself to others having a lease in the same building.

Headlessor – The freeholder.

Holding over – Where the tenant is said to "hold over", this refers to the statutory right to remain in possession with security of tenure at the expiry of a long lease.

Hope value – Usually intended to mean extra value attributable to a reversionary interest where there is a likelihood of being able to negotiate lease extensions to the tenants at some time in the foreseeable future.

Indenture – Nothing to do with teeth, this is an archaic term referring to any sealed agreement and traditionally the term used to refer to a lease.

Initial notice – This is usually used in relation to a notice served under Section 13 of the 1993 Act, being a collective enfranchisement claim in respect of a block of flats as provided for in Chapter I, Part I of the 1993 Act. It may also refer to a notice served under Section 42 of the 1993 Act, this being an individual claim for a 90 year lease extension.

Injurious affection – Where a landlord has more than one property and is required by a statutory claim to sell one of those properties, injurious affection is the damage to any remaining properties that may have been deleteriously affected by the sale.

"Ipse dixit" valuation – This is a valuation which is not supported by evidence, but is reliant purely on the opinion of the valuer proposing it.

Land Registry – The government body set up in 1862 to simplify conveyancing by maintaining a register recording details of interests in land and providing purchasers with a guarantee of good title. The Central London Land Registry Office is at 32 Lincoln's Inn Fields, London WC2.

Lands Tribunal – This is the appeal tribunal which is now known as the "Upper Tribunal (Lands Chamber)" – see below.

Leaseback – An arrangement whereby the landlord sells his interest subject to a new lease to himself in respect of part or all of the property.

Leasehold – Defined in law as a *"term of years absolute"*, it is any tenancy which derives from a lease.

Leasehold Valuation Tribunals – There are 12 Leasehold Valuation Tribunals throughout England and Wales which were established in 1980 to hear applications relating to 1967 Act claims. Their remit was greatly extended both by the 1993 Act and by legislation giving them authority to hear disputes relating to service charge disputes and rights to manage. They are now known as First Tier Tribunals.

Licence – A licence may be created as a deliberate device to avoid a letting being treated as a tenancy in law. Whether or not a licence is distinguished from a tenancy will depend *de facto* on the actual circumstances regardless of whatever the agreement may purport to be.

Long tenancy – A tenancy defined in both the Landlord and Tenant Act 1954 and the Leasehold Reform Act 1967 as having a term of more than 21 years.

Marriage value - When a lease is created in respect of any property, the ownership of that property is split between the freeholder and the leaseholder. The two types of ownership can more easily be seen as rights. The freeholder has the right to collect ground rent and to have the property back at the end of the lease, subject to any statutory provisions relating to security of tenure. The tenant on the other hand has the right to occupy the property for the term of the lease. The aggregate open market value of those two interests is usually less than the open market value of the property as an unencumbered freehold and that difference is the marriage value.

Modern Ground Rent – Defined in Section 15(2) of the Leasehold Reform Act 1967, it is an integral part of a Section 9(1) valuation. The valuation assumption is that the freeholder should receive the full rental value of the site at the expiry of the lease for a term of 50 years subject to one mid-term review only.

Negative marriage value – This occurs in a valuation where the values ascribed to the current freehold reversionary interest and the occupational freehold interest exceed the unencumbered freehold value. It is usually the consequence of attributing values which incorporate prospects of marriage, whereas such valuations should exclude this element.

"No Act World" – This refers to the provisions in both the 1967 Act and 1993 Act where it is necessary to calculate marriage by reference to the value of the existing leasehold interest. In order to avoid double counting, the leasehold interest has to be valued excluding any benefit attributable to the statutory right to enfranchise. In other words, it has to be valued as though the Act did not exist.

Nominee purchaser – With collective enfranchisement there can only be one purchaser of the freehold interest. It is therefore necessary to consolidate the participating tenants into one nominee purchaser. It is most likely that the nominee purchaser will be a company.

Overriding lease – In most circumstances the term "overriding lease" is likely to refer to the headlease covering a block of flats which will therefore be the immediate landlord to the individual underlessees in the building. However, the Landlord and Tenant (Covenants) Act 1995 has a more specific definition in Section 19, providing that if the existing tenant defaults on payments of rent or service charge and the landlord serves a former tenant or guarantor with notice under Section 17 requesting payment, then the party making the payment is entitled to an overriding lease. The party taking the overriding lease would become the direct tenant of the landlord and the immediate landlord of the defaulting existing tenant.

Pannel's valuation method – This is a rarely encountered method of valuing a leasehold interest when there are different tranches of profit rent. Rather than using dual rates of interest, which would result in a mathematical error, the valuation is calculated using single rates. The answer is then adjusted by multiplying the conclusion by the YP based on appropriate dual rates and dividing it by the single rate YP already applied.

Peppercorn rent – A legal euphemism meaning there is no rent to pay. Another more colourful example of this sort of eccentricity would be a red rose on Midsummer's day.

Poll Tax – The popular term for Community Charge (see above).

Profit rent – The difference between rent receivable and rent payable.

PV of £1 – The PV stands for "present value". It is an investment valuation table which computes the value today of a lump sum receivable in the future.

Quarter days – 25 March, 24 June, 29 September and 25 December. These are the days when rent payable quarterly is usually due. The quarterly months are easy enough to remember. The actual days can be remembered due to the coincidence that March has five letters (25), June has four letters (24), September has nine letters (29) and December is on Christmas day.

QC - This stands for "Queen's Counsel" and is a title given to barristers who have reached a certain level of seniority. They are also known as "silks", which derives from the silk gowns that they are entitled to wear in court when they attain this position. However, it should not be assumed that all the best barristers are QCs. Barristers have to apply to be a QC and many extremely eminent barristers have chosen not to make the application.

Rack rental value – The full open market rental value of a property. Since the Housing Act 1988 this may be assumed to be on the basis of an Assured Shorthold Tenancy.

Rateable value – Until replaced by the Community Charge in 1990, and since then by the Council Tax, all residential properties had rateable values determined by the Inland Revenue, from which local taxes could be derived. These were virtually equivalent to the open market rental value of a property held on a fully repairing and insuring basis as at a fixed valuation date, the last one being 1 April 1973. Rateable values and charges relating to them are still applied to commercial properties as a significant part of local government revenue.

Although rateable values are no longer used as a means of raising Local Government revenue from residential property, the old rateable values are still relevant to determine whether a tenant has security of tenure at the expiry of a lease and to determine which valuation basis applies in the case of an enfranchisement valuation of a house.

Regulated tenancy – This is a tenancy that is regulated by the Rent Act 1977. Rent Act tenancies have not been created since 15 January 1989.

Relativity – A term increasingly used in relation to the valuation of a leasehold property where a certain unexpired term may be valued as a percentage of its equivalent freehold value. For example, a 30-year term may be valued "at a relativity to freehold" of 58%. A useful reference for this is *www.GraphsofRelativity.co.uk*

Rent Assessment Committee – This is the committee that hears appeals relating to rental determinations made by the Rent Officer Service.

Registered tenancy – This is a tenancy which is registered with the Rent Officer Service, which is a public office that fixes, where applicable, a "fair rent" in accordance with the Rent Act 1977 and also the open market rent for Assured Periodic Tenancies (see above).

Reversion – That time in the life of a freehold interest when the lease runs out and when the property reverts to the freeholder.

Reversionary – A term used to describe a rent which, having been fixed some time ago, is now at less than the full rental value of a property. Also a "reversionary lease" is one which begins on the expiry (or reversion) of another existing lease.

Section 15 rent – The same as "Modern Ground Rent" (see above).

Secure tenancy – Originally introduced in the Housing Act 1980, they are now governed by the Housing Act 1985 and relate to public sector housing. Various types of public sector landlord may apply and the tenant must occupy the premises as his principle, if not sole, residence. The degree of security of tenure is similar to that afforded by the Rent Act 1977.

Severance – Related to "injurious affection" (see above), a severance payment may be warranted in certain circumstances where, after a compulsory acquisition, a landlord is left with two or more parcels of land whose value has been adversely affected due to the transaction.

Strata title – This term derives from Australian law and is the basis of Commonhold. It is based on the legal right to possession of a lateral part of a property.

Stucco - A sturdy type of plaster used on exterior walls, first introduced at the beginning of the nineteenth century and most famously seen in Belgravia and Pimlico.

Sub-underlease – This is a lease which has been granted by someone having an underlease.

Term – An equivocal word in property meaning either the length of a lease or one of the obligations of that lease.

Tone of the list – An expression used in relation to rateable values where all properties are valued as at the same valuation date so as to ensure an equal "tone". Although rateable values were abolished for residential property in 1990, it still necessary to consider historic rateable values from the 1963 and 1973 Lists in considering the valuation basis under the 1967 Act and in pursuing a Schedule 8 application (see above).

Underlessee – A lessee whose landlord is the tenant of the freeholder. It is the same as a sub-lessee, although the prefix "sub" is more correctly applied to a sub-underlessee (see above).

Unencumbered freehold – This is a freehold title which is not subject to any leases, liens or other encumbrances. A tenant enfranchising the lease of his house may be regarded as acquiring the unencumbered freehold, although this will not be strictly true where there is an estate management scheme (see above).

Upper Tribunal – More correctly known as the "Upper Tribunal (Lands Chamber)" this is the tribunal, previously known simply as the Lands Tribunal that, in the context of leasehold enfranchisement legislation, has heard appeals from First Tier Tribunals since their creation in 1980, when they were known as Leasehold Valuation Tribunals.

Valuation list – This is the list of rateable values prepared by the Inland Revenue. The General Rate Act 1967 required the Revenue to arrange revaluations every 5 years, but it took them 10 years to revise the 1963 list and 17 years to revise the 1973 list. Following the abolition of rateable values on residential property in 1990, the District Valuers Office has managed to carry out revaluations every five years. Historic rateable values on residential property are still relevant in determining the valuation basis for a house under the Leasehold Reform Act 1967.

Virtual freehold – A lease which is so long and contains covenants which are so undemanding they may be considered to be the next best thing to freehold. Usually virtual freehold leases are granted for 999 years at a peppercorn.

Yield – The annual income provided by an investment, usually expressed as a percentage of its cost or its current value. It has become fashionable in recent years to use the word "rate" instead of yield, as in a "deferment rate". They mean the same thing.

VP – Stands for "year's purchase". It derives from an investment valuation table and is a method of attributing a capital value to an income flow by the application of a capitalisation yield.

White knight investor – This is a phrase often used in relation to a collective enfranchisement claim. It occurs where there are non-participants. In such circumstances, there are three options: 1) The participating lessees can agree to pay for the non-participating reversions; 2) The landlord can agree to take a leaseback; or 3) A third party can agree to pay for these non-participating reversions. That third party is termed a "white knight investor". As the lessees will be acquiring the freehold, and there can only be one freehold per building, the white knight investor will need to contend with a 999 year lease in the same way that a landlord would who has agreed to take a leaseback. That white knight investor will then be the "competent landlord" (see definition above) to those lessees who did not participate in the acquisition of the freehold.

The Author

Charles is a Fellow of the Royal Institution of Chartered Surveyors, having qualified in 1982. Since 2002 his practice has been Boston Radford, the Radford name deriving from brothers, Simon Radford and David Radford, who have both been work colleagues for more than twenty-five years.

Charles began specialising in the voluntary surrender and renewal of residential leases in 1978. He soon began dealing with statutory claims and started his own practice in May 1983 under the name Boston Gilmore. Since this time he has acted for well over a thousand clients.

Charles also has a long standing relationship with legal publishers, Sweet & Maxwell. This began in 1986 with a commission to write a concise guide under the title "Understanding Residential Leases". In 2001 Sweet & Maxwell decided to create a new title to add to their prestigious Handbook series to be called "Handbook of Residential Tenancies" and Charles was asked to be the Valuation Editor. He is now the Chief Editor.

In 1992 he was part of a committee advising the Council of Mortgage Lenders on what was to become the Leasehold Reform, Housing and Urban Development Act 1993. In 2001 he was again consulted by the CML in regard to what became the Commonhold and Leasehold Reform Act 2002.

He has been a keynote speaker at professional conferences organised by Henry Stewart Conference Studies, IBC Legal Studies & Services, Kingston University, The Royal Borough of Kensington and Chelsea, Ad Idem Seminars, CLT Conferences and Sweet & Maxwell.

Charles is married with three adult step children and two dogs. He works both from his home in Dorset and an office in central London. In his spare time he enjoys walking in the countryside and playing golf. He is also a prolific singer-songwriter with seven critically acclaimed albums and two UK Country Radio Awards. He regularly plays gigs in a bluegrass style in the West Country (www.CharlieBoston.com).

Boston Radford's website is www.BostonRadford.com and Charles may be contacted at the following:

M: 07740 950 067

E: CB@BostonRadford.com

9 780953 096220